WALTHER P. MICHAEL

THE OHIO STATE UNIVERSITY

MEASURING

INTERNATIONAL CAPITAL

MOVEMENTS

OCCASIONAL PAPER 114

NATIONAL BUREAU OF ECONOMIC RESEARCH

NEW YORK 1971

Distributed by COLUMBIA UNIVERSITY PRESS

NEW YORK AND LONDON

Relation of the Directors to the Work and Publications
of the National Bureau of Economic Research

1. The object of the National Bureau of Economic Research is to ascertain and to present to the public important economic facts and their interpretation in a scientific and impartial manner. The Board of Directors is charged with the responsibility of ensuring that the work of the National Bureau is carried on in strict conformity with this object.

2. The President of the National Bureau shall submit to the Board of Directors, or to its Executive Committee, for their formal adoption all specific proposals for research to be instituted.

3. No research report shall be published until the President shall have submitted to each member of the Board the manuscript proposed for publication, and such information as will, in his opinion and in the opinion of the author, serve to determine the suitability of the report for publication in accordance with the principles of the National Bureau. Each manuscript shall contain a summary drawing attention to the nature and treatment of the problem studied, the character of the data and their utilization in the report, and the main conclusions reached.

4. For each manuscript so submitted, a special committee of the Board shall be appointed by majority agreement of the President and Vice Presidents (or by the Executive Committee in case of inability to decide on the part of the President and Vice Presidents), consisting of three directors selected as nearly as may be one from each general division of the Board. The names of the special manuscript committee shall be stated to each Director when the manuscript is submitted to him. It shall be the duty of each member of the special manuscript committee to read the manuscript. If each member of the manuscript committee signifies his approval within thirty days of the transmittal of the manuscript, the report may be published. If at the end of that period any member of the manuscript committee withholds his approval, the President shall then notify each member of the Board, requesting approval or disapproval of publication, and thirty days additional shall be granted for this purpose. The manuscript shall then not be published unless at least a majority of the entire Board who shall have voted on the proposal within the time fixed for the receipt of votes shall have approved.

5. No manuscript may be published, though approved by each member of the special manuscript committee, until forty-five days have elapsed from the transmittal of the report in manuscript form. The interval is allowed for the receipt of any memorandum of dissent or reservation, together with a brief statement of his reasons, that any member may wish to express; and such memorandum of dissent or reservation shall be published with the manuscript if he so desires. Publication does not, however, imply that each member of the Board has read the manuscript, or that either members of the Board in general or the special committee have passed on its validity in every detail.

6. Publications of the National Bureau issued for informational purposes concerning the work of the Bureau and its staff, or issued to inform the public of activities of Bureau staff, and volumes issued as a result of various conferences involving the National Bureau shall contain a specific disclaimer noting that such publication has not passed through the normal review procedures required in this resolution. The Executive Committee of the Board is charged with review of all such publications from time to time to ensure that they do not take on the character of formal research reports of the National Bureau, requiring formal Board approval.

7. Unless otherwise determined by the Board or exempted by the terms of paragraph 6, a copy of this resolution shall be printed in each National Bureau publication.

(Resolution adopted October 25, 1926, and revised February 6, 1933,
February 24, 1941, and April 20, 1968)

CONTENTS

TABLES

ACKNOWLEDGMENTS

This study was undertaken in connection with the National Bureau's research project on Measuring Transactions Between World Areas. My special thanks go to Herbert B. Woolley, director of the project, who aroused my interest in the quantitative aspects of international transactions and gave me constant encouragement.

I should like to acknowledge with thanks the comments by the members of the staff reading committee, Hal B. Lary, Ilse Mintz, and Michael Michaely, and the Directors' reading committee, Frank W. Fetter, Walter D. Fisher, and Theodore O. Yntema, as well as the helpful comments received from John R. Meyer. I am grateful also for valuable suggestions on an earlier version of this study by Professors Arthur R. Burns, Albert O. Hirschman, and Peter B. Kenen. The latter, particularly, contributed much by his incisive criticisms.

Poul Høst-Madsen and John S. Smith and the staff of the Balance of Payments Division of the International Monetary Fund gave generously of their time in providing information on the data. Samuel Pizer and Eugene S. Kerber, formerly of the Balance of Payments Division of the U.S. Commerce Department, also were most generous in providing me with essential data, as was Frederick Cutler of the Commerce Department. To all of these, my sincere appreciation. The manuscript was skillfully edited by Virginia Meltzer, who also saw it through production.

WALTHER P. MICHAEL

SUMMARY

The purpose of this study is to construct integrated accounts of international capital flows, including grants, between individual countries by type of capital. The basic data on capital movements are the balance-of-payments data reported to and published by the International Monetary Fund. These data were supplemented by estimates from other sources for transactions not covered by the IMF. The period chosen for this exercise was the five years, 1950 to 1954, for which the reported data were sufficiently detailed to undertake this project. The flows of capital and grants between all countries and nonterritorial organizations are covered, with the exception of the transactions between the countries of the Soviet Bloc and communist Asia. The countries were divided into four groups by level of economic development: Group 1 includes the industrial countries, Group 2 the other advanced countries, Group 3 the more advanced underdeveloped countries, and Group 4 the least developed countries.

The reported balance-of-payments statistics on capital transactions, when aggregated into global or area totals, reveal considerable disagreements between changes in assets and changes in liabilities (and between grants extended and grants received); these remain when the estimates of the accounts of the nonterritorial organizations and of countries not covered by the IMF data are added. In order to arrive at fairly accurate estimates of the flows it is, therefore, necessary to ascertain the sources of these discrepancies and to reconcile the statistics as far as possible. For this purpose, the transactions reported by each country were broken down by type, and the data of the partners to each type of transaction were compared. In cases where no breakdown by type of transaction was available in the balance-of-payments statistics, the composition of the flows was identified from partner data or other sources. These comparisons revealed the extent of the discrepancies between the data of each two partners and usually in which type of capital they occurred.

The discrepancies in the global and area totals were found to be largely due to the failure of countries to report certain transactions, or whole types of transactions, which their partners reported, and not the result of some systematic bias. Often, the country that omitted the transaction could be identified, and its account was then adjusted accordingly. If the country could not be identified, no adjustment could be made, and the reported amount remained unallocated. However, the reporting country often identified the area, or groups of countries, with which the transaction took place. The amount could then be allocated to a group, even though unidentified by country. However, discrepancies were also found in many cases where both sides reported the transaction but disagreed on the amount. These discrepancies are due to time lags in reporting or to different calculations underlying the reported figures. Inadequate coverage (or overestimates) may also be involved in some cases, but frequently this could not be discerned.

Although the figures from both sides were taken into consideration, the matrix tables presented in Appendix B for each type of capital show only one figure for transactions between any two partners: if there was agreement, or the discrepancy was removed by an adjustment, there was only one figure; if the discrepancy could not be reconciled, the more reliable figure was taken, but the discrepancies with the partner's figures were recorded and, except when negligible, are given in the notes to the matrix tables. Amounts not allocated by country were included and, as far as possible, assigned to the groups of countries with which the transactions took place (if there were unallocated amounts on both sides presumably covering the same transactions, the larger of the two was taken).

The final estimate of the total supply of capital and grants, net of repayments, exceeds by more than 20 per cent the totals of changes on both the asset and the liability side of the balance-of-payments data as reported to the IMF. The major part of the excess is accounted for by estimates of transactions of nonterritorial organizations and of countries without balance-of-payments reports. Additions for transactions omitted in the reported data were, however, also substantial.

While adjustments for nonreported amounts were necessary in many records, the Continental European countries (called Continental OEEC during this period) were found to be the one group that most seriously understated its capital transactions, particularly the amounts supplied. Apart from the adjustments made in the records of these countries individually, there are also a great many transactions in balance-of-payments reports allocated to the Continental OEEC area as a group (but not identifiable by country), and these exceed substantially the unallocated amounts in the records of these countries that could cover the same transactions. Because of these unallocated amounts, the extent of underreporting can be measured only for the Continental OEEC countries as a group; namely, by counting both the adjustments made in the accounts of the Continental OEEC countries and the amounts allocated to the Continental OEEC group in all records in excess of the corresponding unallocated amounts in the records of the Continental OEEC countries. Measured in this way, the Continental OEEC group accounts for 85 per cent of the total understatement of the reported net increase in assets (including grants extended), and the group understated the gross amounts of the capital it supplied by 43 per cent. These deficiencies in reporting, largely revealed by partner data, occurred not only in transactions of the OEEC countries with each other and with other advanced countries, but also in transactions with many underdeveloped countries.

There is some indication that the deficiencies of the Continental OEEC records are not unique to this early period. An IMF study of discrepancies in balance-of-payments statistics during the early 1960's found that total net capital outflows reported by the member countries of the Organization for Economic Cooperation and Development (OECD) fell considerably short of total net inflows from the OECD reported by all countries. These results are consistent with our findings. Since we found the records of the other countries that became OECD members to be fairly complete (some deficiencies in the United Kingdom record were removed in 1958), it seems that the Continental countries still understated the amounts they supplied in more recent years. The presumption that the statistics of the capital suppliers have better coverage of capital transactions than those of the underdeveloped countries is not borne out for the Continental countries by our findings.

The results regarding the distribution of capital for the five years are shown in the summary Table 1, covering all types of capital, and in Matrix Tables I to VII in Appendix B, which show the flows of each type of capital between individual countries. The bulk of all capital was provided by the industrial countries (Group 1), and among these the United States was the largest supplier. Since postwar reconstruction still played a considerable role during the years 1950–54, the larger part of government capital was in the form of aid to advanced countries, mainly to those in Group 1. The advanced countries also attracted by far the greater part of private investment, although it was Group 2 in this case that received the largest share—almost one-half of total investment. The underdeveloped countries represent, however, two-thirds of the world population (excluding the Soviet Bloc and communist Asia), and Group 4 alone makes up one-half, while Group 2 accounts for only 6 per cent. On a per capita basis the receipts of Group 2 were thus the highest, not only of private capital but of government capital as well; per capita receipts declined with per capita income, Group 4 receiving the smallest amounts of both investment and aid. There were considerable differences, it is true, between the per capita receipts of various regions within groups. Receipts of government aid by the countries close to the communist blocs in Southeast Europe and the Far East were relatively high. Likewise the receipts of the colonies were substantial, particularly those of the French territories, since French colonial aid was especially large. But, measured per capita, receipts of both aid and investment by most of the independent underdeveloped countries, particularly those of the populous countries in Southern Asia, amounted to only fractions of the receipts of Group 2.

The pattern of capital movements whose main features have been briefly indicated here covers only the period of the early 1950's. For a more thorough analysis a longer period would be required. A continuation of this study would, therefore, be desirable. The data for later years have been improved in many respects, and much additional information in supplementary sources has become available, which should facilitate the identification of capital flows. On the other hand, it still appears that the records of some of the main suppliers, the Continental European countries, are inadequate in coverage. The procedure employed in this study, involving a detailed comparison of the country data by type of capital, will be necessary also in deriving estimates for later years. This paper demonstrates that, by this method, it is feasible to reconstruct international capital transactions in matrix form showing the flows by sources and destinations.

MEASURING
INTERNATIONAL CAPITAL
MOVEMENTS

1

PURPOSE AND SCOPE
OF THE STUDY

It is well known that the reported data on international capital movements as given in balance-of-payments statistics are incomplete. When international capital transactions reported by individual countries are aggregated into area or global totals, large discrepancies are found between changes in assets and the corresponding changes in liabilities, or between net outflows and corresponding net inflows. This was found to be the case during work on the National Bureau's study of world trade and payments for the period 1950–54.[1] It is also true of the data for the late fifties and the early sixties, as two recent International Monetary Fund (IMF) studies show.[2] It is, therefore, difficult, if not impossible, to ascertain from balance-of-payments statistics the approximate magnitudes of world capital movements and of the flows between areas or to judge the relative shares of the various suppliers and recipients and the relative importance of the various types of capital.

Moreover, existing studies of postwar capital movements do not contain global quantitative presentations of all flows between countries. The main compilations of capital flow figures are in the United Nations studies of private capital and of grants and long-term capital, and in the publications of the Organization for Economic Cooperation and Development (OECD) on the flow of financial resources to less developed areas.[3] The UN studies of private capital were mainly

[1] Herbert B. Woolley, *Measuring Transactions Between World Areas*, New York, NBER, 1966.

[2] Marcus Diamond, "Trends in the Flow of International Private Capital, 1957–65," *Staff Papers*, International Monetary Fund, March 1967; and John S. Smith, "Asymmetries and Errors in Reported Balance of Payments Statistics," *Staff Papers*, IMF, July 1967.

[3] United Nations, *The International Flow of Private Capital, 1946–1952*, New York, 1954, and *1956–1958*, New York, 1959, and *International Flow of Long-Term Capital and Official Donations, 1951–1959*, New York, 1961, *1959–1961*, New York,

designed to bring out the characteristics of, and some of the factors influencing, private capital flows. While they contain much valuable information, quantitative evidence is confined to the main suppliers and selected recipients. The OECD data cover the supply to the underdeveloped areas of both official and private capital from 1956 on, as reported by the OECD members. The distribution of official capital among recipient countries is also provided from 1960 on, but much less information is given about the distribution of private capital. The scope of the OECD publications is thus limited mainly to the flow of aid to underdeveloped countries. The UN publications on long-term capital and grants cover the same field (although they show only net figures), but they also include data on aid by communist countries. Diamond's IMF study of private capital supplies no breakdown for the recipient countries. Presentations of worldwide capital movements are, therefore, not available.

It is, then, the purpose of this paper to try to construct, out of balance-of-payments data and supplementary sources, a reasonably firm and integrated set of accounts of international capital flows. The method used is to disaggregate the data by type of capital as far as possible and to compare transactions between partners by type. Sufficient details are available in most records or subsidiary sources to make such comparisons between countries, or at least between areas, feasible. In this way the discrepancies between countries or areas are revealed by type of capital. The data can then be adjusted for omitted transactions on the basis of partner data or other sources. The method of comparing the disaggregated data from both sides for all types of transactions seems indispensable for a reasonably accurate estimation of capital transactions. This two-valued approach affords a test of the data that is lacking when only the data of the lenders are used for compilations. Even if the types of transaction between two partners (say, direct investment and portfolio investment) are separately shown in only one of the records, the total amount for "private long-term" in the other still provides a limited check of the data. Of course,

1963, *1960–1962*, New York, 1964, *1961–1965*, New York, 1966; OECD, *The Flow of Financial Resources to Countries in the Course of Economic Development, 1956–1959*, Paris, 1961, *1956–1963*, Paris, 1964, and annual issues, and *Geographical Distribution of Financial Flows to Less Developed Countries*, Paris, 1966.

transactions that took place but are not reported by either side—for instance, Latin American capital flight to Switzerland—or transactions for which neither partner collects data cannot be brought to light. But at least discrepancies in the reported data can be ascertained by this method, and frequently the source of the discrepancy can be identified. Such discrepancies are likely to be quite substantial, and while there may be no way to estimate certain clandestine movements, it is considered useful to reconstruct the movements that can be known. Many transactions that escape exchange control data, where this is the basis for collection, can be caught in the record of the other partner. It is hoped that this aspect of the study, the identification of discrepancies in the data, will prove of value in itself, both for improvement of the reporting system and as a caveat for the use of the figures.

The time period chosen for this purpose is the five years from 1950 through 1954, inclusive.[4] The data reported to the IMF prior to this period were not detailed enough for this kind of study.

The distribution of the supply of capital by source and its allocation among recipient countries are of particular interest with regard to the level of development of the countries between which the flows occurred. Accordingly, a classification of countries by stage of development has been constructed in order to show capital flows between such groups of countries, and how the various types of private and official capital were distributed among them.

The results of the investigation are given in summary form in Table 1 and in a series of matrix tables, found in Appendix B, for major types of transactions cross-classified by source and destination of funds. These tables are for the five-year period as a whole. Though the procedure followed has involved a year-by-year inspection of the data, the preparation of annual matrixes would have increased both the burden of work and the uncertainties of the estimates without a commensurate gain in knowledge of the period studied or in experience relevant to the feasibility of developing systematic accounts of this nature in the future.

This study focuses on the exposition of the methodology and the problems that are encountered in constructing a matrix system of

---

[4] This study was undertaken in connection with the National Bureau project mentioned in footnote 1, which covers the same period.

TABLE 1
Total Capital Movements, Types of Capital, by Groups and Subgroups, Five-Year Totals, 1950–54
(millions of dollars)

Borrowers (recipients)	Total	Group 1	U.S.	U.K.	Continent and Japan	Group 2	Canada	Other Group 2	Group 3	Group 4	International Institutions	Unallocated
						Lenders (donors)						
TOTAL	40,280	35,015	21,057	3,340	10,618	1,750	1,097	653	209	2,094	1,057	155
I. Government grants and net loans	17,228	16,078	12,649	732	2,697	−16	−223	207	12	−91	1,243	2
II. Portfolio investment issues	3,044	2,981	1,610	713	658	63	43	20	34	24		42
Portfolio redemptions and trading	−657	−516	−762	84	162	−241	−90	−151	−10	8		90
III. Direct investment	11,492	10,601	6,865	2,459	1,277	803	623	180	−7	−7		21
IV. Private loans, net	222	264	378	−60	−54	−49	4	−53	−7	−57		
V. Repatriations	−627	−563	−56	−399	−108	−2		−2	−5			
VI. Short-term credit^a	2,365	2,219	214	−33	2,038	456	409	47	10		−320	
VII. Reserves,^b correspondent accounts, and net quota payments to international institutions	7,213	3,591	159	−156	3,948	736	331	405	175	2,217	134	
GROUP 1	17,155	14,133	8,650	435	5,048	1,167	944	223	178	1,829	−233	81
I. Government grants and net loans	6,681	7,036	7,067	−140	109	−250	−242	−8	2	−79	−30	2
II. Portfolio investment issues	70	70			70							
Portfolio redemptions and trading	201	353	19	223	111	−265	−102	−163	34	29		50
III. Direct investment	2,792	2,189	1,128	428	633	581	548	33	−5	1		26
IV. Private loans, net	3	24	261	−63	−174	−11		−11	−6	−7		3
V. Repatriations	−84	−51		−11	−40				−1	−32		
VI. Short-term credit	816	758	40	121	597	409	409				−351	
VII. Reserves^b and correspondent accounts	6,676	3,754	135	−123	3,742	703	331	372	154	1,917	148	

U.S.											
	7,170	4,713	601	4,112	1,297	1,082	215	348	401	336	75
II. Portfolio investment issues	17	17		17							
Portfolio redemptions and trading	364	377	246	131	-104	-94	-10	31	10		50
III. Direct investment	1,402	864	391	473	521	512	9	-6	1		22
IV. Private loans, net	11	10	2	8	-2	-2	-2				3
V. Repatriations	-2								-2		
VI. Short-term credit	414	48	48		366	366					
VII. Reserves[b] and correspondent accounts	4,964	3,397	-86	3,483	516	298	218	323	392	336	
U.K.											
	3,139	2,571	2,294	277	-161	-96	-65	-193	1,337	-415	
I. Government grants and net loans	1,189	1,481	1,472	-11	-191	-191		-4	-77		
II. Portfolio investment, redemptions, and trading	-183	-8	-8	-173	-10	-163			-2		
III. Direct investment	621	573	527	46	48	30					
IV. Private loans, net	143	152	168	-16	-9	-9					
V. Repatriations	-28								-28		
VI. Short-term credit	146	401		43	43	43				-298	
VII. Reserves[b] and correspondent accounts	1,251	-8	135	121	32	89	-65	-189	1,444	-117	
Continent											
	5,966	6,045	5,629	657	29	-44	73	23	91	-228	6
I. Government grants and net loans	4,975	5,069	5,089	120	-59	-51	-8	6	-2	-41	2
II. Portfolio investment issues	53	53		53							
Portfolio redemptions and trading	37	1	39	-20	12	2	10	3	21		4
III. Direct investment	659	644	501	113	10	4	6	1			
IV. Private loans, net	-227	-214	18	-167				-6	-7		
V. Repatriations	-54	-51		-40				-1	-2		
VI. Short-term credit	62	178	-18	196						-116	
VII. Reserves[b] and correspondent accounts	461	365	-37	402	66	1	65	20	81	-71	

(continued)

TABLE 1 (continued)

Borrowers (recipients)		Lenders (donors)										
	Total	Group 1	U.S.	U.K.	Continent and Japan	Group 2	Canada	Other Group 2	Group 3	Group 4	International Institutions	Un-allocated
GROUP 1 (continued)												
Japan	880	804	727	75	2	2	2				74	
I. Government grants and net loans	517	506	506								11	
II. Portfolio investment, redemptions, and trading	-17	-17	-12	-5								
III. Direct investment	110	108	100	7	1	2	2					
IV. Private loans, net	76	76	75		1							
VI. Short-term credit	194	131	58	73							63	
GROUP 2	8,539	8,010	5,350	1,595	1,065	99	11	88	-1	4	375	52
I. Government grants and net loans	1,825	1,443	1,073	191	179	-30	-8	-22	-1	-4	417	
II. Portfolio investment issues	1,673	1,653	1,179	385	89	20	1	20				
Portfolio redemptions and trading	-498	-497	-535	-34	72	10	1	9		4		-15
III. Direct investment	5,126	4,973	3,616	1,088	269	101	14	87		4		48
IV. Private loans, net	59	82	51	-4	35	-42	4	-46				19
V. Repatriations	-13	-13		-13								
VI. Short-term credit	415	387	-58	23	422	47		47			-19	
VII. Reserves^b and correspondent accounts	-48	-18	24	-41	-1	-7		-7			-23	
U.S.-oriented	4,846	4,855	4,268	174	413	-6	4	-10		-4	-8	9
I. Government grants and net loans	574	585	370	84	131	-18		-18		-4	11	
II. Portfolio investment issues	1,165	1,165	1,165									
Portfolio redemptions and trading	-376	-366	-407	-44	85	2		2				-12
III. Direct investment	3,388	3,386	3,070	186	130							2
IV. Private loans, net	88	44	53	-12	18	10	4	6			19	
VI. Short-term credit	48	44	-7	1	50						4	
VII. Reserves^b and correspondent accounts	-41	-18	24	-41	-1						-23	

U.K.-oriented	2,572	2,131	582	1,387	162	125	13	112		8	308
I. Government grants and net loans	584	255	229	24	2	5		5			324
II. Portfolio investment issues	449	449	14	371	64	28	2	26			
Portfolio redemptions and trading	51	23	-52	49	26	98	11	87		4	-4
III. Direct investment	1,379	1,273	372	846	55	1		1		4	4
IV. Private loans, net	71	70	19	43	8						
VI. Short-term credit	45	61		54	7						
VII. Reserves [b] and correspondent accounts	-7					-7		-7			-16
Continent-oriented	1,121	1,024	500	34	490	-20	-6	-14	-1	43	75
I. Government grants and net loans	667	603	474	83	46	-17	-8	-9	-1		82
II. Portfolio investment issues	59	39		14	25	20		20			
Portfolio redemptions and trading	-173	-154	-76	-39	-39	-20	-1	-19		1	
III. Direct investment	359	314	174	56	84	3	3	-53		42	
IV. Private loans, net	-100	-47	-21	-35	9						
V. Repatriations	-13	-13		-13		-53					
VI. Short-term credit	322	282	-51	-32	365	47		47			-7
GROUP 3	4,930	4,266	3,247	-157	1,176	283	50	233	3	7	369
I. Government grants and net loans	2,716	2,233	1,805	131	297	185	-18	203		3	297
II. Portfolio investment issues	10	10	10			9	9				
Portfolio redemptions and trading	-202	-213	-92	-120	-1	87	59	28	-5	4	1
III. Direct investment	1,444	1,357	1,238	40	79	4		4			-1
IV. Private loans, net	127	124	45	7	72	-2		-2	-2		
V. Repatriations	-165	-163	-55	-77	-31						
VI. Short-term credit	1,000	918	296	-138	760				10		72
U.S.-oriented	2,335	1,973	1,768	-276	481	99	66	33	-5	4	262
I. Government grants and net loans	683	476	453	23		-2	-2				209
II. Portfolio investment issues	10	10	10			9	9				
Portfolio redemptions and trading	-173	-184	-80	-110	6	87	59	28	-5	4	
III. Direct investment	1,373	1,286	1,185	40	61	5		5			
IV. Private loans, net	150	146	65	7	74						
V. Repatriations	-122	-122	-55	-67							
VI. Short-term credit	414	361	190	-169	340						53

(continued)

TABLE 1 (*concluded*)

Borrowers (recipients)	Total	Group 1	U.S.	U.K.	Continent and Japan	Group 2	Canada	Other Group 2	Group 3	Group 4	International Institutions	Unallocated
GROUP 3 (continued)												
Continent-oriented	2,595	2,293	1,479	119	695	184	−16	200	8	3	107	20
I. Government grants and net loans	2,033	1,757	1,352	108	297	187	−16	203	−2	3	88	
II. Portfolio investment, redemptions, and trading	−29	−29	−12	−10	−7							
III. Direct investment	71	71	53		18							
IV. Private loans, net	−23	−22	−20		−2	−1		−1				
V. Repatriations	−43	−41		−10	−31	−2		−2				
VI. Short-term credit	586	557	106	31	420				10		19	
GROUP 4	7,982	7,422	3,109	1,324	2,989	82	33	49	8	171	279	20
I. Government grants and net loans	5,231	4,884	2,334	437	2,113	47	32	15	13	−14	301	
II. Portfolio investment issues	647	647		295	352							5
II. Portfolio redemptions and trading	−39	−36	−47	18	−7	1	−1	2		−9		15
III. Direct investment	2,130	2,082	883	903	296	34	2	32		−1		
IV. Private loans, net	33	34	21		13				−1			
V. Repatriations	−365	−336	−1	−298	−37				−4	−25		
VI. Short-term credit	117	139	−81	−39	259						−22	
VII. Reserves [b] and correspondent accounts	228	8		8						220		
U.S.-oriented	2,088	1,973	1,908	−18	83	−8		−8	−1	4	99	21
I. Government grants and net loans	1,516	1,424	1,416		8	−8		−8		4	96	
II. Portfolio investment issues	2	2			2							
II. Portfolio redemptions and trading	−19	−19	−16	−3								
III. Direct investment	619	598	581	1	16							21
IV. Private loans, net	30	31	19		12				−1			
V. Repatriations	−17	−17	−1	−16								
VI. Short-term credit	−43	−46	−91		45						3	

U.K.-oriented	2,780	2,409	929	1,376	104	89	34	55		156	125	1
I. Government grants and net loans	1,354	1,173	728	437	8	55	32	23		-22	148	
II. Portfolio investment issues	295	295	295	295	5	1	-1	2		-9		5
Portfolio redemptions and trading		3	-28	26	35	33	3	30		-1		-4
III. Direct investment	1,188	1,160	235	890	1	33	3	30		-21		
IV. Private loans, net	2	2	1		1							
V. Repatriations	-303	-282	-259	-259	-23					-21	-23	
VI. Short-term credit	27	50	-7	-21	78				-4	209		
VII. Reserves[b] and correspondent accounts	217	8	17	8	136				11			
Continent-oriented	3,114	3,040	272	-34	2,802	1	-1	2	9	11	55	-2
I. Government grants and net loans	2,361	2,287	190		2,097				13	4	57	
II. Portfolio investment issues	350	350		350	350							
Portfolio redemptions and trading	-20	-20	-3	-5	-12							
III. Direct investment	323	324	67	12	245	1	-1	2				-2
IV. Private loans, net	1	1	1	1								
V. Repatriations	-45	-37		-23	-14				-4	-4		
VI. Short-term credit	133	135	17	-18	136						-2	
VII. Reserves[b] and correspondent accounts	11								11	11		
INTERNATIONAL INSTITUTIONS	1,342	1,131	677	108	346	104	59	45	21	86		
I. Government grants and net loans	446	426	348	78	147	18	13	5		2		
II. Portfolio investment issues	644	601	421	33		43	43					
Portfolio redemptions and trading	-100	-103	-92	-3	-8	3	3	7				
VII. Reserves (IBRD bonds)	81	10			10	7		7	22	42		
Net quotas	271	197			197	33		33	-1	42		
UNALLOCATED	332	53	24	35	-6	15		15		-3	267	
I. Government grants and net loans	329	56	22	35	-1	14		14		1	258	
II. Portfolio investment, redemptions, and trading	-19	-20	-15	-5	-5	1		1				
VI. Short-term credit	17	17	17									
VII. Reserves[b] and correspondent accounts	5	17		-4						-4	9	

a Partly net, see (4), below.

b Excluding gold.

NOTE: A minus sign indicates a decrease in assets (liabilities).

SOURCE: Derived from matrix tables for Types I to V, and VII. The magnitudes of I, II, and VII differ from those of the corresponding matrix tables because of changes explained in (1), (2), (3), and (5) below. The flows of Type VI (for which there is no matrix) were calculated from the data in Appendix Table B-VI and from reported (or adjusted) country data, as explained in (1) and (4) below.

(1) In order to simplify the exposition in this summary table, the European Institutions were eliminated as intermediaries for grants and EPU balances. The grants extended *to* EPU and IEPA (EPU and IEPA rows in Appendix Table B-I) were distributed among the groups in proportion to the grants made *by* these institutions (EPU and IEPA column in Appendix Table B-I), which reduces the total of Type I by $700 million. The EPU balances (Appendix Table B-VI, column 3) were treated as having been extended directly by the countries with credit balances to those with debit balances, viz., by Group 1 Continent to itself, the United Kingdom, Group 2 (net of Swedish credit balance), and Group 3 (net of Portuguese credit balance). The credit balances of Sweden and Portugal were treated as having been extended to their own groups. The EPU net receipt was included in Group 1. The eliminated balances extended by EPU amount to $920 million (the sum of the debit balances). For their loan transactions (Appendix Table B-I), the European Institutions were included as lenders in the Continent-Japan column, and as borrowers in the Continent row. The total magnitude is not affected in this case.

(2) International Bank for Reconstruction and Development (IBRD) bonds bought by central banks as reserves are included in both Appendix Tables B-II and B-VII because from the borrower's point of view they represent funds raised through security issues, while from the lenders' point of view they represent an increase in their reserves. Either matrix would thus be incomplete without these transactions. But to avoid double counting in this summary table, the amount was excluded from Type II ($81 million).

(3) IBRD sales of borrowers' obligations included in Appendix Table B-II (portfolio trading) were transferred here to Type I, since they constitute a reduction in the supply of the International Institutions (−$67 million).

(4) Short-term credit (Type VI) was calculated for this table as explained below. For Groups 2, 3, and 4, the net receipts (or net repayments) were shown as having been received from (or repaid to) Group 1 in the following way: Their net receipts from (or repayments to) the U.S. and the U.K., according to the U.S. and U.K. data, were entered in the respective columns, and their residual transactions were entered in the Continent-Japan column, with the following exceptions:

(a) The Canadian transactions with the U.S. and the U.K. were shown gross since they largely consist of Canadian credit extended rather than received. The Canadian asset figures were used for this purpose.

(b) The EPU balances were treated as described above.

(c) The currency transactions with the International Monetary Fund (IMF) were shown as liabilities to the International Institutions.

(d) For Group 3, U.S.-oriented (Group 3 Latin America), the British figure of the Latin American repayments to the United Kingdom was used, the residual receipts from the Continent and Japan becoming, therefore, correspondingly larger (see Walther P. Michael, "International Capital Movements, The Experience of the Early Fifties (1950–1954)," Ph.D. dissertation, Columbia University, 1965. Appendix B, Matrix IX, 1).

The net credit extended by the Group 1 lenders to each other was shown in the following way:

(a) U.S. column—The net credit received from the United States by the Group 1 Continent and Japan according to the data of these countries was entered.

(b) U.K. column—The net credit received by the United States ($48 million) and Japan ($73 million reported by Japan) was entered.

(c) Continent and Japan column—Since the OEEC countries in Groups 2 and 3 reported net inflows from the Continental OEEC area totaling approximately $350 million, an offsetting net repayment was entered under Group 1 in this column because we estimated (see Michael, *ibid*.) that the net increase in short-term indebtedness in the whole Continental OEEC area was approximately zero. This negative entry was reduced by $65 million for the net credit extended to the United Kingdom according to the data of these Group 1 countries. The Continental-Japanese transactions, which were relatively small and unidentifiable by group, were ignored.

The sums of these various estimates yielded then the total for Group 1 of $2,219 million, and for all Short-Term Credit, of $2,365 million (this total is smaller by $920 million than the final estimate of $3,285 million shown in Table 2 because of the eliminated EPU balances). By this procedure we have assigned the missing outflows, evidenced by the discrepancy in Appendix Table B-VI, to Group 1 Continent (see the notes to Appendix Table B-VI). We have also included any transactions between the other groups in the Continent-Japan column, but such transactions were generally small and net out to insignificant amounts. The (partial) gross figures in this table for Group 1 cannot be reconciled with the net figures in Appendix Table B-VI because of the treatment described above, but those for Groups 2, 3, and 4 are consistent with the net figures in Appendix Table B-VI. This procedure seems to yield the best possible approximation to the short-term credit flows which appear to have taken place.

(5) Net quotas (the net increases in the liabilities of the International Institutions on subscription account), for which no matrix is included (see Chapter 2, footnote 4), were added to Type VII ($271 million).

---

world capital movements.[5] However, in Chapter 4 the pattern of capital movements during 1950–54 is discussed and some conclusions regarding the flow of funds to the underdeveloped areas are drawn.

[5] The methodology is explained here in general terms. For the procedure used in particular estimates and for the adjustments made to the reported country data, see Walther P. Michael, "International Capital Movements, The Experience of the Early Fifties (1950–1954)," Ph.D. dissertation, Columbia University, 1965 (microfilmed).

2

COVERAGE AND SOURCES

Coverage of Transactions

The study embraces all capital transactions and nonmilitary official grants among all countries except members of the Sino-Soviet Bloc. The items covered are those reported during this period to the International Monetary Fund under the four categories of the capital account (official and private, each divided into long-term and short-term) and under official donations (nonmilitary grants by governments and international institutions). The inclusion of official grants is customary in studies of this kind.[1] Foreign aid consists of both grants and loans, and the distinction is tenuous in many cases, since loans have sometimes been converted to grants, or grants to loans, and since some loans carry only nominal interest or are interest-free.

Since, in principle, all capital transactions are covered in this study, short-term credits and changes in foreign currency reserves are included. Short-term credits have been of considerable importance in the supply of financial resources to some developing countries. Accumulations of currency reserves may also be drawn upon in lieu of other capital imports, and were so used by a number of countries. Moreover, the substantial increase in world currency reserves that occurred during the 1950–54 period meant large inflows for the United States and the United Kingdom, modifying their gross capital exports to some areas considerably. To obtain a complete picture of world capital flows, these movements must, therefore, be included.

On the other hand, this coverage is arbitrary in some respects. Three other items might have been partially or wholly included, but their exclusion is unavoidable. (1) The exclusion of military grants is cus-

---

[1] The OEEC/OECD studies have, for instance, the same coverage for all but short-term movements. In studies of "foreign investment," on the other hand, grants are omitted. See, e.g., Raymond F. Mikesell, ed., *U.S. Private and Government Investment Abroad*, Eugene, Ore., 1962.

tomary, as for instance in the *Balance of Payments Yearbooks* of the International Monetary Fund. While it may be debatable whether they should be included, sufficient details are not divulged. (2) If official donations are included, it might appear that private donations should also be included, but, again, the available data are not adequate for the purpose. (3) The definition of direct investment (part of private long-term capital) as newly raised capital plus reinvested profits [2] is somewhat arbitrary. The expansion of plant and equipment takes place also through the use of depreciation and depletion allowances. Their source is the same as that of reinvested profits, namely earnings, but the division between them depends to a considerable degree on tax laws and is, therefore, in an economic sense arbitrary. Direct investment does not, therefore, fully reflect the real gross investment that took place, but that is unavoidable.

Types of Transactions

To be able to observe differences in the distribution of government aid, private investment and loans of various kinds, and short-term capital flows, we have distinguished seven types or groups of transactions and have constructed a table for each one (called matrix tables) showing transactions between individual countries. There are asymmetries in the classification of reported data on loan capital because some transactions are reported as "private" on one side and as "official" on the other—for instance, bond issues if the borrowers are governments, or official loans if they are made to private borrowers. Since the motives of governments differ from those of private lenders, and since the distribution of long-term capital is largely determined by the lenders, the distinction between "government" and "private" loans in this study is made on the lenders' side. For short-term capital the distinction between liquid claims and credits seemed to be more useful for our purpose, and more feasible, than that between official and private flows. The seven types of capital distinguished here are listed on the following page.

---

[2] From the point of view of the balance of payments, reinvested profits do not, of course, represent capital flows. But in this study they have been included because the use of profits for investment, no less than the use of remitted funds, results from the decisions of the investors.

Type I. Government Grants and Loans. This group consists of grants and loans (net of repayments) made by governments, or their agencies, and by international institutions. It includes International Bank for Reconstruction and Development (IBRD) loans, grants and loans made by or through the intermediary of the European payments organizations, the Intra-European Payments Agreement and the European Payments Union (IEPA and EPU), and UN grants.[3]

In the matrix, grants and loans are listed separately, though qualifications regarding this distinction have been noted above. Grants are not necessarily "aid" but include reparations and some other contractual payments. Loans include some providing for the delivery of strategic materials to the lending government.

Type II. Portfolio Investment. Here new issues floated in foreign markets are distinguished from trading in securities and redemptions. The latter two elements cannot be separated from each other, however, since redemptions are indistinguishable from ordinary market transactions in many cases.

Type III. Direct Investment. As indicated above, reinvested profits are included wherever possible. Where this could not be done for lack of data, the fact is mentioned in the notes to the table, and the possible distorting effect on the pattern of direct investment is discussed.

Type IV. Private Loans. Under this heading, loans by commercial banks and industrial or other business concerns are covered. They are largely intermediate-term loans.

Type V. Extraordinary Repatriations. These are return flows from borrowers to lenders or investors reported, or otherwise distinguishable, as repatriations of capital due to nationalization, compensation for previously nationalized enterprises, or sales of enterprises and other assets in the wake of independence of a number of countries.

Type VI. Short-Term Credit. Short-term credit represents the residual after elimination of changes in official reserves and in banks' corre-

---

[3] The term "government" was used rather than "official" to avoid confusion with the IMF usage of "official" which included, during this period, commercial banks.

spondent accounts from total short-term movements (changes in claims with maturities of one year or less). In addition to ordinary trade credits, it includes changes in payment agreement balances and other payments arrears (i.e., movements which represent, in effect, credits, although they were not formally extended as such).

For short-term credit a matrix could only be constructed according to the IMF area system because in many of the accounts the country detail could not be ascertained. This matrix served only to infer the approximate pattern of the flows and is not reproduced in this study. Appendix Table B-VI shows instead the net inflows and outflows by country without source and destination, and the direction of the flows is discussed in the text. In the summary given in Table 1, the flow of short-term credit between groups is shown partly on a net basis (see the notes to Table 1).

Type VII. Reserves and Correspondent Accounts. These transactions cover changes in liquid assets, i.e., the international currency reserves of monetary authorities and working balances of commercial banks (including the sterling balances of some business concerns not separately shown). Gold flows, being part of reserve changes, but not part of capital flows, are included in Table B-VII in a separate column, but are excluded from the summary table.

Sufficient detail is available in balance-of-payments reports or other sources to make the foregoing classification feasible. There are comparatively few transactions that do not clearly fall under one of these headings; after inspection, either these were allotted to one or another of the matrixes, or their exclusion was indicated.[4]

The Design of an Area System

In order to relate the distribution of capital flows to levels of economic development, it was necessary to devise a suitable system for

[4] An eighth type of transaction is represented by the quota payments of new IMF and IBRD members and the resulting increases in holdings of member currencies by these institutions. Since these transactions are of little interest, they have not been reproduced in tabular form. The net contributions by the members to the institutions have been included, however, in the summary table. These consist of the increases in the countries' long-term assets (quotas) minus the in-

grouping countries.[5] For this purpose, countries were divided into four groups according to stage of development. Within these groups, they were further classified into subgroups according to their main trade-orientation toward one of three centers, viz., the United States, the United Kingdom, and the Continental OEEC countries.[6] This area system is shown in Appendix Table A.[7] The division into four groups was based on the following criteria.

DIVISION OF COUNTRIES INTO NET EXPORTERS AND
NET IMPORTERS OF INDUSTRIAL GOODS

Historically the main capital suppliers have been the industrial countries. There are many reasons for this. Suffice it to say that to a large degree foreign investment has been related, directly or indirectly, to the financing of exports of industrial products and of imports of raw materials needed for industrial enterprises. The division of countries into net exporters of industrial goods and those that are not is, therefore, relevant in our context.[8] Nine countries were found to be net exporters of industrial goods: United States, United King-

creases in the countries' short-term liabilities (domestic currency subscriptions). These net amounts are equal to the dollar and gold subscriptions, which result in corresponding changes in the reserves of the members and the institutions (Type VII).

[5] The area system employed by IMF for the balance-of-payments reports of this period is a mixed geographical and currency-area system. Included in the same areas are countries of very different economic structures and stages of development, and the system is, therefore, not suitable for our purpose.

[6] The division by trade-orientation was developed by Woolley. See Herbert B. Woolley, *Measuring Transactions Between World Areas*, New York, NBER, 1966, Chapter 5, Table 5-1.

[7] The country and area designations used in Appendix Table A and elsewhere in this study refer to the period 1950–54. Rhodesia consists of the federation of Southern Rhodesia, Northern Rhodesia (now Zambia), and Nyasaland (now Malawi). The European Overseas Territories include those countries that were dependencies at the time.

The matrix tables cover, in addition to the countries in Appendix Table A, the then existing nonterritorial organizations engaging in capital transactions: UN, IBRD, and IMF, which are referred to in this study as "International Institutions"; and IEPA, its successor (July 1, 1950), EPU; BIS, and ECCS, which are called the "European Institutions."

[8] Industrial goods were taken to mean SITC classes 5 (chemicals), 7 (machinery and transport equipment), and 6 and 8 (other manufactured goods). The calculation was based on the data in the United Nations' *Yearbook of International Trade Statistics, 1955*. It was made for the aggregates of the years 1953 to 1955, for which the SITC classification is available for the first time in convenient form for a number of countries. Data for Japan were available only for 1954 and 1955.

dom, Austria, Belgium-Luxemburg, France, Germany, Italy, Switzerland, and Japan.

Two countries generally considered industrial countries, the Netherlands and Sweden, were net importers of industrial goods. For the nine countries named above industrial exports not only exceeded industrial imports but they were also more than 50 per cent of their total exports, and industrial imports were, with the exception of Switzerland (54 per cent), less than half of their total imports. The Netherlands conforms more closely to this pattern than Sweden. For the Netherlands, industrial imports were less than 50 per cent of total imports, industrial exports were 48 per cent of total exports, and it was a net exporter of chemicals. Also Benelux as a whole was a net exporter of industrial goods. The Netherlands was, therefore, included in the industrial net exporter group. Sweden, on the other hand, conforms only in that its industrial exports exceeded 50 per cent of total exports. It is also convenient to keep Sweden with the other Scandinavian countries. Sweden was, therefore, not included in Group 1 but rather in Group 2. The nine net exporters of industrial goods plus the Netherlands form Group 1.

DIVISION INTO GROUPS BY PER CAPITA INCOME AND
AGRICULTURAL SECTOR

The net importers of industrial goods were divided into three groups according to economic levels as evidenced (directly) by per capita income and (inversely) by the relative size of the agricultural sector,[9] the latter variable being measured both by the percentage of the adult male labor force in agriculture and by the percentage contribution of agriculture to total product.[10] The reasons for using all three of these measurements are, first, for a number of countries only one or the other set of data is available; second, they provide a useful check on each other, since these data are known to have weaknesses; and, third, any one by itself may conceal some characteristic

[9] The negative correlation between per capita income and share of the agricultural sector is well known. See Simon Kuznets, "Industrial Distribution of National Product and Labor Force," *Economic Development and Cultural Change,* July 1957, pp. 8–9 and 20–22.

[10] Based on data for the period of this study; see the statistical notes to Appendix Table A.

that should be given more weight in the classification, as in the case of Venezuela (see note 11 below).

The three groups distinguished on the basis of these criteria have the following characteristics: Group 2 includes the other high income countries with agricultural sectors similar to those in Group 1; Group 3 includes the more advanced underdeveloped countries generally with per capita incomes of $200 to $250 and agricultural labor force proportions between 40 and 50 per cent; Group 4 includes the least developed countries with per capita incomes ranging from $160 downward and labor force proportions in agriculture generally of 60 per cent or more. The dependencies were included in Group 4 in toto (although some of them may belong to Group 3) because the capital movements cannot be broken down for them individually.

For some countries no data are available on the three criteria. But these countries are unquestionably among the least developed and have been included in Group 4. The one exception is Uruguay whose economic level was assumed to be similar to that of Argentina, and it was therefore included in Group 2. In some cases that do not conform to the general pattern, it seemed advisable to rely on only one or another of the criteria as the basis for classification.[11] In summary, Groups 1 and 2 include the advanced countries, Groups 3 and 4, the underdeveloped areas.

Sources and Nature of the Data

Our main source is the balance-of-payments data on capital movements and official donations reported by member countries and some nonmembers to the International Monetary Fund and published in the Fund's *Balance of Payments Yearbook*.[12] The rules for classifica-

---

[11] Thus, Venezuela was placed in Group 3 on the basis of its relatively large agricultural sector (since the high per capita income reflects mainly the high productivity of the oil industry); Iceland was included in Group 2 on the basis of its high per capita income (because the relatively large "agricultural labor" percentage is inflated by the inclusion of fishing); and South Africa and the Rhodesian Federation were included in Group 2 because of the small agricultural sectors for the European populations (that of Southern Rhodesia in the case of the Federation).

[12] IMF, *Balance of Payments Yearbook*, annually. The Yearbooks covering the period 1950–54 are: Vol. 5, 1947–53, Washington, D.C., 1954; Vol. 6, 1953–54, Washington, D.C., 1955; Vol. 7, 1954–55, Washington, D.C., 1956; Vol. 8, 1950–54, Washington, D.C., 1957.

Our data differ from those of the Yearbooks mainly because of adjustments and supplementary estimates made by us. Some unpublished revisions were incorpo-

tion of transactions and for the regional breakdown in the balance-of-payments reports are laid down in the Fund's *Balance of Payments Manual*.[13] According to this guide, capital transactions were reported during this period by changes in assets and liabilities under four major headings: private long-term, private short-term (items 11–14 in the Yearbook), official long-term, and official short-term (items 15–18). Long-term is defined as claims or investments with an initial maturity of more than one year or without maturity. Short-term claims are those of one year or less, or payable on demand.[14] Official capital includes, for the period covered by this study (and until 1960), the operations of commercial banks in addition to the transactions of governments and official bodies. These headings are further broken down by the more important types of transactions, and it is these breakdowns that we used for our classification. Grants are reported as official donations (item 10).[15]

The regional classification called for by the Fund's Manual distinguishes the United States, the United Kingdom, Canada, Rest of Sterling Area, Continental OEEC countries (substituted for the original Western Europe), Latin America, and Rest of the World (or Other Countries). The dependencies are shown separately, and some of the areas are further subdivided into smaller groups.[16] If this classification is observed in every detail by the reporting country, the transactions with the two most important countries in international finance, the United States and the United Kingdom, are revealed, although for the transactions with the rest of the world (except Canada) only the partner areas, and not individual countries, are known. However, since capital movements are not as widely dispersed as current account transactions, there are usually only a limited number of possible part-

rated, however, in this study. On the other hand, Vol. 8, which carries revised data for the period but without regional distributions, includes a number of revisions of which only the more substantial could be incorporated.

[13] IMF, *Balance of Payments Manual*, 2nd ed., Washington, D.C., 1950, which was the guide for this period. With the third edition (1960) the classification of the capital account and the requirements for regional details were changed.

[14] *Ibid.*, pp. 5–6.

[15] Those data that were not reported in U.S. dollars were converted at the official par rates given in the country sections of the IMF Yearbooks. In the case of Canada, for which no par rates had been established, the annual average rates were used, given in the Canadian section of the Yearbooks. For Syria and Lebanon, where transactions took place at various free rates, the free dollar rates were used.

[16] *Op. cit.*, p. 76, Table A.

ners within an area to the transactions of a given country. Moreover, breakdowns of types of capital or identifications of particular transactions by country are frequently available. Thus, it is possible to identify a great many types of transactions by country, at least on one side, from the reported data.

Supplementary data are published by a number of countries. The United States publishes breakdowns of most of its transactions. Further details were obtained through the courtesy of the staff of the Balance of Payments Division of the U.S. Commerce Department. The U.S. movements could therefore be identified, with minor exceptions, both by type of capital and by country. Moreover, since the transactions of the United States comprise the larger part of the world's capital movements, a great many transactions reported by other countries without adequate regional distribution could be identified with the help of the U.S. data.

Much less additional information was available for the United Kingdom and the Continental European countries. Their official transactions could generally be identified from the reported data. British private investment was, however, reported only net, in one item including all types of private movements, with a regional distribution, which is unreliable.[17] The Bank of England published for this period an annual series, *United Kingdom Overseas Investments*, with country breakdowns. These data, however, were of very limited use because they cover only fractions (ranging from one-tenth to one-third) of the (net) investment that took place according to the U.K. balance of payments. They cover only securities issued in the U.K., the U.S., and Canada, and, therefore, leave out all direct investment in the form of intercompany account entries, intermediate-term loans, and reinvested profits, which is usually the major part of direct investment flows. (The coverage is also incomplete in other respects.) Government bonds and loan and share capital of private companies are distinguished at nominal values, but the cash value of investment or disinvestment is shown only for all securities combined. These data were useful mainly in cases of transactions where, according to other evidence, only portfolio investment was involved and the cash figures were thus meaningful. But the data were not adequate for a

---

[17] See the discussion of the U.K. account below in Chapter 3.

reconstruction of total private investment or even all portfolio transactions. Another source, the *Midland Bank Review,* provided, however, annual data on security issues in the London market from which, in conjunction with partner data, these issues could be estimated.

The French balance-of-payments publication supplies country breakdowns of gross inflows and outflows, distinguishing between official and private, and between long- and short-term, but not by types of capital. Since this distribution is also based on currencies, it is of use mainly for soft-currency countries. The transactions with the overseas territories are not included, however, and had to be estimated from OEEC publications.

Thus, transactions of the European capital exporters had to be identified largely on the basis of information available for the capital importers.[18] In this respect foreign investment censuses and breakdowns in balance-of-payments publications of the major sterling countries and some others generally supplied the information to establish the direction, magnitude, and composition of the European flows to these countries. A number of monographs on Latin American countries published by the U.S. Department of Commerce yielded similar information on European investment in Latin America.

Information was also obtained from the *International Financial News Service,* published by the Fund (mainly on loan transactions), and from the British bank reviews, the London *Economist,* and other financial news sources.

[18] Perhaps this is because countries with younger statistical offices follow the Fund's reporting rules more closely than countries that have long collected data according to their own rules.

3

THE DATA

Preparation of the Data for the Construction of Matrixes

METHODOLOGICAL APPROACH

First, "trial-run" matrixes were constructed, according to the IMF area system, in order to ascertain the extent of the disagreements between the reported data. For this purpose, the country data were combined into area totals with area distributions.[1] Changes in assets of each area were entered in the columns, and changes in liabilities in the rows, of the trial-run matrixes. Each cell thus represents the transactions between a pair of areas and shows the change in assets reported by one and the change in liabilities reported by the other. If all reports were accurate, these two figures should show reasonably close agreement.

Discrepancies were found, however, in virtually all cells, some of considerable size. Indeed, in several cases there was disagreement about the direction of capital flows (i.e., whether there was an increase or a decrease in assets and liabilities). Although there were unallocated amounts, these could not account for most of the discrepancies. As a matter of fact, if distributed among the areas, they operated in some cases to make the discrepancies larger. No systematic bias could be discerned in the discrepancies, which might have made uniform adjustments possible. Further checks revealed that numerous specific transactions, or whole types of transactions, were left out from one side or the other, and that some regional distributions were suspect. It also became apparent that close agreements in some cases were spurious, because they were partly the result of accidental agreements

[1] Some preliminary adjustments to the data were made for this purpose on the basis of partner data, viz., transactions known to be omitted on one side were added and figures reported on a net basis were converted into gross changes in assets and liabilities.

between amounts representing different types of transactions. In brief, it became evident that a reconstruction of capital flows could not be based on one set of data alone (say the lenders' with perhaps some supplementary estimates), but that the matrixes had to be built up from both sides. The procedure involved, therefore, a detailed examination of all country records and comparisons by types of transactions, and even comparisons of individual transactions, for all years.

After this initial appraisal of the data, the next step was to construct country accounts by types of capital distributed by partner countries and areas. Breakdowns by types of capital and by partner country, where not reported, were made from partner records or other sources, and adjustments were made for nonreported transactions. Complete reconciliation could not be achieved, however, because unallocated amounts remained, and because partner records frequently disagreed on the amount of a given type of transaction (e.g., direct investment), or even that of a specific transaction (e.g., a loan). Since, in such a case, the reason for the disagreement was not known, a reconciliation was not possible and a discrepancy remained.[2] Thus, a choice had to be made between partner figures. If the capital flow originally had been completely identified in only one of the records, that figure was chosen for the matrix. Where the flow was identified on both sides and one of the figures inspired more confidence than the other, it was chosen. But in some cases more or less arbitrary judgments had to be made. Moreover, to the extent that the comparison between partner data provides a test of their accuracy, the discrepancy between them is an indication of the possible margin of error. All remaining discrepancies were, therefore, recorded and, except those that are small in relative or absolute terms, are commented upon in the notes to the matrix tables.

Some country accounts had to be constructed exclusively from partner data or from other sources because no balance-of-payments reports existed. For others the reported data required major reorganization or supplementary estimates. The majority of the accounts, however, could be compiled more or less directly from the reported data.

[2] In the case where an account was adjusted for an omitted transaction from partner data no discrepancy remains, of course; if the adjustment was based on another source, however, the estimate may not agree with the partner figure, and in that case there is a discrepancy.

CONSTRUCTION OF UNREPORTED ACCOUNTS

New accounts or partial accounts had to be constructed for (a) the Sino-Soviet Bloc and four independent countries, (b) some of the dependencies, and (c) the International Institutions.

(a) The accounts for the Sino-Soviet Bloc and for Spain, Saudi Arabia, Afghanistan, and Nepal were constructed solely from partner data. For the latter four countries the transactions consisted mainly of U.S. aid, investment (in Saudi Arabia), and bank loans (to Spain), and some minor transactions with other countries. It is unlikely that there were other substantial transactions with these countries that are not covered. Soviet Bloc movements reported by partners consisted of Finnish reparations, a large Swedish loan, and smaller loan transactions with a number of other countries. No capital transactions were reported with Mainland China. Changes in the sterling balances of Sino-Soviet Bloc countries could not be identified.

(b) For some of the dependencies, balance-of-payments statements did not exist. The French and Portuguese balance-of-payments data cover only the transactions of their entire currency areas with the rest of the world. The dependencies' transactions with other countries are thus included. But their transactions with France and Portugal (i.e., the data on colonial aid and investment receipts) had to be obtained from other sources. For the French territories, estimates were based on data in OEEC publications and some IMF data.[3] The estimates are necessarily rough. The OEEC data are in themselves estimates and do not cover 1950 and 1951. Data for these earlier years were obtained from other sources or estimated by extrapolation. The figure for the total gross inflow from France over the five-year period ($2.4 billion, of which $1,978 million was in aid and $412 million in private investment) has to be regarded as a rough approximation. The amount is not likely to be overstated, however, since the private component does not include an estimate for reinvested profits. Movements from the territories to France could not be estimated.

For the movements between Portugal and its territories, only data

---

[3] OEEC, *Economic Development of Overseas Countries and Territories Associated with OEEC Member Countries*, Paris, August 1958, mainly Table 44, p. 108; OEEC, *Sixth Report of the OEEC*, Paris, March 1955, Vol. II, Chapter XXVIII, Table 53, pp. 231 and 251–253; and IMF, *Balance of Payments Yearbook*, Vol. 9, Morocco section.

for aid during 1953–54 of $17 million are available,[4] but it seems that the capital supplied by Portugal during the whole period was not much larger.[5] Private investment seems to have been small or negligible.

For two other territories, Dutch and Australian New Guinea, partner data (Netherlands, Australia, and U.S.) were used.

(c) Balance-of-payments accounts for the International Institutions were constructed from data in their publications, particularly *International Financial Statistics* of the IMF and annual reports of the various institutions. In the case of the European institutions, partner data were also used.

REORGANIZATION OF COUNTRY ACCOUNTS

The private capital accounts of the United Kingdom and several Sterling Area countries had to be reorganized or supplemented with additional estimates. The United Kingdom reported its private capital during these years as one net item, distinguishing transactions with the Sterling Area and various other regions. For purposes of this study, these flows had to be broken down into changes in assets and liabilities, by types of capital, and by partner countries. Supplementary British sources served this purpose to some degree as mentioned in Chapter 2 but, very largely, the breakdown was based on partner data (after these accounts had been adjusted or reorganized as described below).

Our breakdown of the U.K. outflow to the Sterling Area of approximately $2.4 billion resulted in very close agreement with the combined Sterling Area (net) receipts, the British outflow falling short of the Sterling Area inflow by $69 million. The U.K. data are said to be based "extensively" on Sterling Area figures,[6] and the data are therefore not independent, but it is doubtful that the underlying calculations are identical to those made here. In any case, the procedure seems to establish the approximate magnitudes adequately.[7]

---

[4] OEEC, *Economic Development of Overseas Countries and Territories, op. cit.,* pp. 190–191, Tables 16 and 18.

[5] *Ibid.,* p. 188.

[6] H. M. Treasury, *United Kingdom Balance of Payments, 1946–1957,* London, 1959, p. 11.

[7] The allocations to the United States made in the various Sterling Area estimates are also generally close to the U.S. figures.

On the other hand, the comparison of the U.K. net flows with the data reported by nonsterling partners revealed large disagreement. The areas that the U.K. distinguishes are the Dollar Area, non-Dollar Latin America, Continental OEEC, and Other. Only in the case of non-Dollar Latin America is there some agreement in that both sides report a net repatriation of capital to the U.K. Although there is still a considerable discrepancy, this may well originate in large unallocated amounts of private short-term capital in the Latin American accounts, particularly in the case of Brazil. For this area we divided the U.K. figure only between long- and short-term, i.e., we identified the long-term transactions from the Latin American records, and assumed the residual to be short-term.

For the other three areas the disagreements are extremely large. The U.K. reports a net inflow from the Dollar Area of close to $1 billion, while according to partner figures the mutual investment flows approximately offset each other. To Continental OEEC and to Other the U.K. reports large net outflows, which these areas do not acknowledge. On the other hand, for the three areas combined, the U.K. figure is approximately zero, and this does agree with the combined partner figures. The explanation for these offsetting discrepancies seems to be that the U.K. private capital figures contain multilateral settlements to such a degree that they distort the capital flows completely.[8] In other words, what appeared as receipts of capital from the Dollar Area were probably, in fact, dollar payments on current account from the other areas. The flows had to be revised, therefore, according to partner figures. The Continental OEEC data are the weakest because of some unallocated amounts. The rearrangement of the U.K. figures for these three areas was, accordingly, made in the following manner: the British entries were made equal to all partner entries except for short-term capital with the Continent, and the residual discrepancy was assigned to that item. This discrepancy is again extremely small. This is the more surprising because the Conti-

---

[8] The private capital item in the U.K. balance of payments for these years is a residual. Estimates of multilateral settlements ("Transfers") are shown, however, and thus eliminated from the regional capital figures. To the extent that these estimates are incomplete, multilateral settlements are still included in the regional capital totals. The possibility of inclusion of multilateral settlements in the capital figures is, in fact, acknowledged (see *ibid.*, p. 14), but the extent seems not to have been realized.

nental figures are probably incomplete and subject to error. But what-
ever is missing must approximately cancel out. In any case, this estimated area distribution seems to reflect the actual movements more
accurately than the reported one.

Other major changes made in Sterling Area accounts were as follows:

(a) Ireland reported net figures (inflows) for the bulk of its private
capital. We identified these movements from various sources and estimated the amounts of the various types of capital involved.[9] The
flows consisted mainly of repatriation of Irish capital from the U.K.
and British purchases of Irish bonds.

(b) Australia reports its balance of payments by fiscal year. The data
were roughly adjusted to a calendar year basis by averaging successive
pairs of fiscal years. In both terminal years the trend of the transactions was upward. The resulting possible underestimate for the first
half of 1950 should, therefore, be at least partly offset by an over-
estimate for the second half of 1954, and the error should be small.

(c) The Indian balance of payments omits all direct investment,
and the estimate used here was derived from Indian census data.[10]

(d) South Africa reports only net inflows, allocated to the Dollar
Area, the Sterling Area, and the Continental OEEC countries. Here
the breakdown was made from 1956 census data.[11] In the estimate the
existence of prewar investment, particularly that of France, was taken
into consideration. For the Union's transactions with other Sterling
Area countries the estimates resulted in a net outflow from the Union
of approximately $50 million to Rhodesia, as well as some minor trans-
actions with countries other than the United Kingdom. Since these
amounts were broken out from the reported net figure, the inflow
from the United Kingdom to South Africa became correspondingly
larger than the reported net figure.

[9] *The Economist*, 1950, Vol. 160, p. 1172; 1951, Vol. 161, pp. 967 and 1389; Vol.
162, pp. 328, 386, and 786; Vol. 163, pp. 88–90; Vol. 164, pp. 742, 775–777, and
781; 1953, Vol. 169, pp. 126 and 479; 1954, Vol. 172, p. 437; Vol. 173, p. 159. Bank
of England, *United Kingdom Overseas Investments*, annual data; and U.S. partner
data.

[10] Reserve Bank of India, *Report on the Survey of India's Foreign Liabilities and
Assets as on 31st December 1953*, Bombay, 1955; *Report . . . 31st December 1955*,
Bombay, 1957.

[11] South Africa Reserve Bank, *The Foreign Liabilities and Assets of the Union
of South Africa, Final Results of the 1956 Census*, Supplemental Quarterly Bulletin
of Statistics, December 1958.

(e) The capital account of the U.K. Overseas Territories, which is only partially reported, was supplemented with estimates based on the error item and U.S. figures.

(f) The petroleum investment in Iraq, which is not reported, was estimated.[12]

These various Sterling Area estimates are, of course, subject to some margin of error, and those made for South Africa and the Overseas Territories are necessarily somewhat rough. But it must be remembered that the total of all the Sterling Area amounts allocated to the United Kingdom corresponds closely to the U.K.'s outflow. The amounts allocated to the United States in these estimates are generally also close to the U.S. figures. We believe, therefore, that these estimates are essentially correct.[13]

ADJUSTMENTS TO COUNTRY ACCOUNTS

Most of the other countries' accounts were reported in a form suitable for direct comparison with partner data, although regional distributions and details by types of capital varied widely.[14] In these comparisons various situations, which are explained below, were encountered.

(a) The transaction, or type of transaction, is completely identified on both sides by amount and country, with agreement or disagreement about the amount. This is the case of most official loans, grants, security issues, many cases of direct investment, and some other transactions. In such cases, no adjustments were made for any discrepancies, which are due mainly to time lags (in case of grants and loans) and different valuations and definitions of direct investment. The U.S. is a partner to the majority of these transactions as lender, and the U.S. figures were chosen for entry in the matrix. A discrepancy, if any, was recorded for the change in the corresponding liability. The U.S. figures were used to achieve consistency in timing and in definition of type of transaction. They also seemed generally more reliable in light of the way in which, for example, some partners described their calculations of direct investment.

[12] I am indebted to Cornelius Dwyer for this estimate.

[13] New Zealand reports by fiscal year ending March 31. In this case no adjustment was made. There is, therefore, the possibility of a discrepancy due to timing.

[14] Belgium, however, reported under private capital only net outflows with a regional distribution based on currencies, except for transactions with the Congo. No basis existed for the breakdowns of the net figures. Their treatment is explained below.

(b) The transaction may be completely identified by one partner, but clearly omitted from the other partner's record. This occurs when all the partner's transactions are identified as something else, or when the partner reports no transactions in categories that could possibly include this amount. In this case, the account was adjusted for the missing item on the basis of the first partner's figures. Cases of omitted direct investment and reinvested profits are the most frequent under this heading. Germany, for example, did not report any private capital until 1953, and Sweden, in all years, reported only small portfolio transactions through Swedish banks. However, both countries received direct investment from the U.S. in all years, both in cash flows and in reinvested profits. Sweden also made direct investments and extended private loans according to various partners' records. Moreover, reinvested profits are often omitted if the report is based on exchange control data. If reinvested profits were specifically excluded, or the acknowledged amount of direct investment approximated only the cash investment of the partner, reinvested profits were added. There were, however, a considerable number of cases where failure to collect certain kinds of data is not the explanation for the omission. A case in point is the repayment by the French Treasury to American banks of $200 million from 1953 to 1955, $103 million of which fell in our period. Although receipt of the loan in 1950 was reported by France, the repayment was not.[15] There were other cases of this sort. In twenty-one instances, accounts were adjusted for government loans or repayments that should have been included in the reported figures.

(c) The item may be identified completely on one side but incompletely on the other. One partner may not distinguish various kinds of private capital, or he may combine repayments of government and bank loans, or combine repayments to several countries. In such cases, identification by type of capital, or country, was made from partner data. Discrepancies, if any, were assigned to the type or country where the largest transaction was involved.

(d) A country identified as the partner to a transaction in the record of another country (say Latin American) may only specify the area (i.e., Latin America). If the amount the country has allocated to Latin

[15] There is the possibility that the repayment found its way into the French short-term capital account. This was found, however, to be unlikely upon a comparison of the French and U.S. official short-term data.

America was approximately equal to the respective amount in the record of the Latin American country, then the entry was assumed to represent this transaction.

(e) Since repayments of commodity loans (official long-term) were often made via payments agreements (official short-term), one partner may show the repayment under long-term, while the other has no corresponding long-term entries. If a comparison of the two short-term accounts revealed that the latter had simply treated the repayments as a reduction in payments agreements balances, then the amount was transferred from short-term to long-term in his account.

(f) In cases of small transactions specified by one country (say small amounts of direct investment, loans, repayments, or portfolio transactions) it may not be clear whether the partner has included them. In these cases the latter's account was neither checked off nor adjusted for this amount, but a discrepancy was recorded. This procedure presents some risk of double-counting, but the amounts involved are too small to affect the distribution materially.

TRANSACTIONS UNIDENTIFIABLE BY PARTNER COUNTRY OR TYPE

In the case of transactions with the Continental OEEC countries often only the area is identified. This is true of the records of the OEEC countries themselves as well as of those of countries outside the area. These amounts could only be entered under "Unidentified OEEC" (as far as they could not be identified from partner data or other sources). However, the reported increases in liabilities to "Unidentified OEEC" exceed by far the unallocated increases in assets reported by the OEEC countries. For direct investment alone (Type III), amounts received from Unidentified OEEC amounted to $469 million, while the change in the corresponding asset figures totals less than $100 million. There are also other unallocated receipts (e.g., direct investment in Israel, Turkey, and other countries) to which the Continental countries must have been largely the partners.

Similarly, for portfolio purchases (Type II) in the U.S., Canada, and the Netherlands by unidentified Continental OEEC countries, there are no unallocated asset entries in the records of the OEEC countries to match them.

For short-term credit (Type VI), the situation is similar. In this case a number of countries report large amounts not allocated even by an area. After all possible adjustments had been made, the sum of the inflows of short-term credit of all countries exceeded the sum of the outflows by more than $1 billion. While the flows could be established here only by approximate magnitudes, we inferred from the area pattern that the discrepancy was largely accounted for by credits extended by the Continental OEEC countries but not reported by them.[16] There are also a number of long-term export loans (Type IV) to Latin American countries extended by, but not reported by, the Continental countries.

While thus a considerable number of transactions had to be left unallocated in the matrixes, the majority of the unidentified lenders were the Continental OEEC countries. The number of possible lenders is, therefore, small, and one can be confident that they fall largely or entirely into Group 1.

The origin of the disagreement on transactions to which the Continent was a partner must be sought in the records of the Continental countries. The transactions not included by them, but reported by their partners, are generally sufficiently identified by type of capital and in other respects to dispel any doubt that they took place. Failure to report these transactions seems to be partly a result of reliance on exchange control data that do not cover such items as reinvested profits, for which no foreign exchange is required. Data for export credits, both intermediate- and short-term, were generally not collected. Some incomplete records—for example, that of Switzerland—are no doubt mainly responsible for missing portfolio transactions and some direct investment. The lack of detail in some of these reports also makes it difficult to ascertain just what is included and what is not.

The lack of detail or the incomplete coverage in the Continental OEEC reports created some other problems that could not entirely be solved. The Swiss account was compiled by the IMF, and it is most useful as far as it goes, but it excludes all movements that cannot be revealed under Swiss Law, direct investment, and small transactions that are not published. Sweden reports only some portfolio transactions for private capital. Belgium has only net figures (outflows)

---

[16] As mentioned in Chapter 2 (Type VI), the area matrix from which this inference was drawn is not reproduced in this study. For the explanation, see Walther P. Michael, "International Capital Movements, The Experience of the Early Fifties (1950–1954)," Ph.D. dissertation, Columbia University, 1965 (microfilmed), Appendix B, Matrix IX (1).

for all private capital without any breakdown by type and, except for transactions with the Congo, a regional distribution by hard and soft currencies that cannot be used. France has also a currency distribution but with a country breakdown (except for the Sterling Area) that seems to largely represent transactions with the countries specified, except for those allocated to the United States. The latter seem to cover all transactions in U.S. dollars and include receipts under private long-term assets amounting to $210 million that, according to partner data, did not come from the United States. Also, France has no identification by type of capital. The Dutch private long-term transactions and the German private long-term liability item are broken down by type for total transactions only, while the German asset item is unidentified by type. The records of these six countries caused the main problems encountered in this study, and the identification of their private long-term transactions brought most of the difficulties.

Two kinds of movements seem to be involved. The first are official or semiofficial repayments of accumulated trade balances or other claims. Such repayments constitute an important part of the intra-European transactions of that period. They are usually identified as government transactions under official long-term and were included in Appendix Table B-I. For some repayments of this kind reported by the Netherlands and Switzerland, however, no corresponding receipts can be identified under official long-term. On the other hand, there are the large private long-term dollar receipts by France that almost certainly must include receipts of such repayments because there seems to be no repatriation of private investment of that magnitude. The Dutch and Swiss official repayments were therefore assumed to correspond to the French private receipts and were included under Type IV (private loans and repayments) since the division between private and official loan transactions is based on the asset side. A part of the Belgian private outflow was also assumed to correspond to the French receipts and included under Type IV, as mentioned below. For such intra-European repayments the dividing line between Types I and IV is, therefore, somewhat blurred. It is also possible that the French receipts and the Belgian outflow contain other types of capital as well (and possibly involve areas other than the Continental OEEC, although that is unlikely for the French receipts).

Second, in the French and a few other records there are some transactions, allocated by country or area, that clearly represent private capital but are not identified by type. In such cases the most likely type of capital was chosen for each transaction (partly on the basis of information contained in the partner's record) to keep the unallocated amounts to a minimum, but these cases are annotated to the effect that they may contain other types of capital. The matrixes involved are II, III, and IV. The possible errors in the allocations to one type or another cannot cause offsetting discrepancies that would distort the magnitudes because the discrepancies involving the OEEC countries are all in the same direction.

Finally, after allocation from partner data of the Belgian net outflow under private long-term, $129 million remained unallocated. Half of this amount was assumed to represent a reduction in liabilities in the form of private loan repayments and was included, as mentioned above, under Type IV; the other half was assumed to be an increase in Belgian assets abroad in the form of direct investment and included under Type III. It was the discrepancies in these two matrixes which indicated that the Belgian outflow mostly included these types of transactions.

Some arbitrariness in the construction of the matrix system was, therefore, unavoidable but it is confined mainly to intra-European (and intra-Group 1) transactions and has little effect on the estimates of flows between groups.

Construction of Matrix Tables

The fact that unallocated amounts and discrepancies between the data remain presents a problem for the construction of matrix tables because there are two total values for each type of capital, one for the total (adjusted) changes in assets and one for the total (adjusted) changes in liabilities (see Table 2). There are two possibilities for presenting such data in matrix form.

(a) The first, the method of presentation chosen here, is to give only one total value for all transactions of a given type by assigning the unallocated amounts, as far as possible, to the group to which they mainly apply and by excluding the discrepancies from the table.[17]

The unallocated amounts, although unidentified by partner country, are usually identified by area, which is often, and for the majority of the larger amounts, the Continental OEEC. In the other cases, which area was the partner can be inferred (usually also the Continental OEEC). We assumed the countries involved to be mainly the Group 1 Continental countries and consequently included these unallocated amounts in this group.[18] Some other unallocated amounts, generally small, were similarly in the groups which were inferred to be mainly the partners. The greater part of the unallocated transactions could thus be included in one or the other of the four groups. There are, of course, unallocated amounts on one side that evidently cover the same transactions as the unallocated amounts reported by the other. To avoid double-counting, only the larger of two corresponding amounts was entered in the table in these cases.

The discrepancies were excluded from the table, but are discussed in the notes to the tables. Many discrepancies are quite small in absolute amounts. They may be in part the result of rounding compounded by currency conversion. In other cases they are small relative to the amounts involved. In such cases generally no detail was provided, while in cases of absolutely and relatively large discrepancies the amounts are specified. (There is generally little chance of large offsetting amounts being concealed in a small discrepancy.)

(b) An alternative solution would be to maintain the two-valued presentation by including not only the unallocated amounts, but also the discrepancies in the matrix table itself in the following manner: Again the lenders appear in the captions, the borrowers in the stub. Each column then shows the amounts supplied by the lender to all

---

[17] In Appendix Table B-VI (short-term credit), which presents only net outflows and inflows of individual countries, the over-all discrepancy is shown, however, since it was assumed to be the unreported net outflow from the Continental OEEC countries to the rest of the world, as mentioned above.

In Appendix Tables B-I to B-V, the lenders (and donors of grants) appear in the captions (and in the columns before the amounts where groups of lenders were combined into one caption), the borrowers (and recipients of grants) in the stub. In Appendix Table B-VII (reserves) the arrangement is reversed because, in contrast to the other types, there are many lenders and only a few borrowers.

[18] Except for some Norwegian transactions where mainly Sweden seems to have been the partner; these were included in Group 2. Otherwise there is no indication in the records of the Group 2 and 3 OEEC countries that they were involved in these transactions as partners.

borrowing countries according to his or the borrowers' data, which-
ever were chosen. At the bottom of each column two further entries
are made if required, viz., amounts reported by the lender that cannot
be allocated by borrower, and any discrepancy between the lenders'
and the borrowers' data, as far as the latter were used. The arithmetic
sum of these two cells thus represents the difference between the
lenders' total supply and the sum of the amounts acknowledged by
the borrowers. For the borrowers, the unallocated amounts and the
discrepancies with the lenders' data, if these were used, appear in the
last two cells on the right of each row. There are then two grand
totals, one each for the total change in assets and the total change
in liabilities, which differ by the total unallocated amounts and discrepancies of one side minus those of the other.[19]

This method of presentation has the advantage that the reader is
immediately informed of the existing discrepancies between the (adjusted) data. But it has the disadvantage of requiring an additional
summary table with only one set of totals for the world and groups
and subgroups before the approximate magnitude of the flows can be
unambiguously shown [the treatment of unallocated amounts and discrepancies in such a table would be the same as explained in (a)
above]. Since the regional distribution in the balance-of-payments reports has become less systematic with the revision of the Fund's
Balance of Payments Manual in 1960, it may be more difficult to
identify unallocated amounts by area and, thus, to assign them to
groups. In that case this alternative method of presentation may be
more feasible for the data of the recent period.

The Deficiencies in the Reported Data

In the preceding sections, it was explained that extensive additions
were made to the reported data and that, furthermore, unallocated
amounts remained, representing transactions which, to a large extent,
were also not reported by the unidentified partners. We consider now
the magnitudes of the reporting deficiencies and in which flows the
understatements occurred. Table 2 shows the additions made to the

---

[19] Showing the discrepancies at the ends of the columns and rows is less cum-
bersome than entering the figures of both partners in each cell since in the many
cases where the figures agree the amounts would be the same, and where they
do not the discrepancy may not be attributable to a single partner but may occur
with the sum of the amounts of several partners.

TABLE 2

Estimates of Total Capital Flows by Types of Capital, Five-Year Totals, 1950–54

(millions of dollars)

| | Estimated Changes in Assets (and extended grants) | | | | Estimated Changes in Liabilities (and received grants) | | | | Net Difference, Excess of Liabilities over Assets (col. 8 minus col. 4) (9) | Final Estimate (10) |
	Originally Reported to IMF (1)	Adjustments — Additions to Increases (2)	Adjustments — Additions to Decreases (3)	Adjusted Estimate (4)	Originally Reported to IMF (5)	Adjustments — Additions to Increases (6)	Adjustments — Additions to Decreases (7)	Adjusted Estimate (8)		
I. Grants	13,871	1,856		15,727	12,676	2,353	−22 [a]	15,007	−720	15,729
Government loans	3,585	2,463		6,048	4,246	1,768		6,014	−34	6,009
Government loan repayments	−3,528		−160	−3,688	3,531		−192	−3,723	−35	−3,743
Government loans, net	57	2,463	−160	2,360	715	1,768	−192	2,291	−69	2,266
II. Portfolio investment issues	2,890	235		3,125	2,160	965		3,125		3,125
Portfolio redemptions and trading	−890	80	−116	−926	−102	13	−221	−310	616	−724
III. Direct investment, flows	9,659	{317 / 806}	{−7}	10,775	7,752	{1,226 / 2,285}	{−33}	11,230	455	11,492
Direct investment, reinvested profits										
IV. Private loans	1,495	54		1,549	1,509	81		1,590	41	1,649
Private loan repayments	−1,205		−82	−1,287	−1,094		−199	−1,293	−6	−1,427
Private loans, net	290	54	−82	262	415	81	−199	297	35	222
V. Repatriations	−657		−16	−673	−506		−87	−593	80	−627
VI. Short-term credit	3,088	2,202	−1,586	3,704	3,752	2,165	−1,015	4,902	1,198	3,285 [b]
VII. Reserves and correspondence accounts	6,147	952	−514	6,585	7,049	452	−285	7,216	631	6,942
Total capital and grants	34,455	8,965	−2,481	40,939	33,911	11,308	−2,054	43,165	2,226	41,710 [c]
Adjustments to reported accounts		3,771	−501			3,487	−709			
Constructed country accounts		300	−200			3,322	−338			
Constructed accounts, nonterritorial organizations		4,894	−1,780			4,499	−1,007			
Total		8,965	−2,481			11,308	−2,054			

NOTES TO TABLE 2

a Return of lend-lease grants.

b Partly net; see note to column 10.

c See note to column 10.

NOTE: *Columns 1 and 5.* These columns show the totals of the amounts reported in the balance-of-payments accounts of all countries included in the IMF *Balance of Payments Yearbooks* covering the years 1950 to 1954. As explained in the text, the original data are not always identified by type of capital, and in a number of cases the figures are reported net. The breakdowns in these columns by type of capital were made after all transactions had been identified and the net figures had been broken up into changes in assets and changes in liabilities.

Columns 2, 3, 6, and 7. The rows below the adjustments by type of capital show to what extent these adjustments consist of (a) additions to the reported country accounts, (b) estimates of transactions of nonreporting countries, and (c) estimates of transactions of nonterritorial organizations. The latter consist of the following: UN, IMF, IBRD, IEPA, EPU, ECCS, and BIS. The row "Adjustments to Reported Accounts" includes all additions made to the reported data of the countries in the Yearbooks, including supplementary estimates in cases where one or two years were not reported, or where the account was only a partial account in other respects.

Column 9. The net differences between the adjusted estimates of changes in assets and in liabilities are equal to the sums of the unallocated amounts and the irreconcilable discrepancies on the liability side minus the sums of the unallocated amounts and discrepancies on the asset side. The discrepancies on the liability side are the differences, if any, between the borrower's figure and that of the lender (or lenders) if the latter was chosen; and conversely in the case of the discrepancies on the asset side.

Column 10. The final estimates include the unallocated amounts but exclude the discrepancies except in the case of short-term credit. In cases where unallocated amounts on the asset side were assumed to cover the same transactions as unallocated amounts on the liability side only the larger of the two amounts was included (usually those on the liability side).

In the case of short-term credit, the discrepancy is the net discrepancy between total net outflows and total net inflows (as given in column 1 of Appendix Table B-VI), and not the sum of discrepancies of transactions between identified partners as is the case in all other types of capital. This discrepancy was assumed to represent mainly the unreported cumulative credits extended by the Continental OEEC countries and it was, therefore, included in the final estimate.

For some types the final estimate exceeds the adjusted estimates of both sides. This occurs when unallocated amounts of both sides are included and/or eliminated discrepancies have a negative sign. In the case of short-term credit the final estimate is smaller than the adjusted (gross) estimate of either side because most of the flows between groups could only be estimated net (changes in assets net of changes in liabilities). The gross total of short-term credit lies between $4.2 and $4.6 billion (see Walther P. Michael, "International Capital Movements, The Experience of the Early Fifties (1950–54)," Ph.D. dissertation, Columbia University, 1965 (microfilmed), Appendix B, Matrix IX, 1), say at $4.4 or $1.1 billion above the figure entered here. A more comprehensive estimate for total capital flows would thus be higher by this amount, viz., approximately $42.8 billion for total capital and grants.

The final estimates for each type of capital are the totals of the matrix tables (except in the case of Type VI, as explained below). They differ, however, from the totals in Table 1 for Types I, II, VI (see below), and VII because in order to simplify the exposition in that summary table, the European Institutions were eliminated as intermediaries, and because of some other changes, as explained in the notes to Table 1.

In the case of Type VI the treatment is different because no matrix table with country detail could be constructed. Since Appendix Table B-VI shows only net outflows and inflows without origin and destination, flows between groups are only shown in the summary table, Table 1, for which partial gross flows were calculated. This calculation involved, apart from some other operations, the assignment of the missing outflows (evidenced by the discrepancy in Appendix Table B-VI) to the Continental OEEC countries of Group 1, and yielded the total of $3,285 million for Type VI shown in column 10 of this table. By eliminating the EPU as intermediary, this amount is reduced by $920 million (the sum of the debit balances in column 3 of Appendix Table B-VI) to $2,365 million, the total shown in Table 1. For a more detailed explanation see the notes to Table 1.

---

original data of each side, the remaining net differences, and the final estimates of each type of capital flow. (For an explanation of the columns, see the notes to Table 2.)

The final estimate (column 10 of Table 2) exceeds the unadjusted totals of both sides (columns 1 and 5) by more than 20 per cent. Neither the supply nor the receipts side of the reported data reflect, therefore, the approximate magnitude of world capital movements adequately. It is also noteworthy that the original totals agree more closely than the adjusted totals, but this agreement is fortuitous because it is due to offsetting discrepancies in the different types. Even if the most obvious asymmetry is removed by adding the transactions of the nonterritorial organizations, the final estimate still exceeds the unadjusted totals by more than 13 per cent. It seems, therefore, hazardous to draw conclusions either about the statistics or the size of flows from aggregative capital flow figures, as is often done, without the disaggregation by types and countries which has been employed here. The larger of the two global totals may still considerably understate the real flows. In that case, estimates of the transactions for which no data are available based on the global discrepancy may be quite misleading.[20] Also, the over-all discrepancy includes not only non-reported transactions but also the discrepancies between reported amounts due to time lags or different methods of estimation by the

[20] See, e.g., Marcus Diamond, "Trends in the Flow of International Private Capital, 1957–65," *Staff Papers*, IMF, March 1967, p. 12, Table 3. Long-term private investment, with which Diamond's study deals, originally showed, for instance, for the 1950–54 period an excess of changes in assets over changes in liabilities of $1.6 billion, while after adjustments liabilities exceeded assets by $1.2 billion.

two partners, which can be considerable. They can be sorted out from the amounts of the omitted transactions only by disaggregation.

We turn now to the question: In which balance-of-payments reports do the deficiencies mainly occur? The breakdown of the total additions to the data in the lower part of Table 2 shows that the major part of the additions consists of estimates of the transactions of the institutions and countries for which no balance-of-payments reports exist. The adjustments to the accounts of the reporting countries were, however, also substantial. While many adjustments were made in all areas, it is the Continental OEEC countries (for all of which balance-of-payments reports existed) that most seriously understated their transactions, mainly on the supply side. The deficiency in the area's reporting is measured by the adjustments made to the OEEC country records plus the amounts in all records allocated to the Continental OEEC, but not identifiable by country (or the excess of these amounts over unallocated amounts in the Continental OEEC records, if any, which seem to cover the same transactions). Measured in this way, the Continental OEEC area accounted for 85 per cent of the total deficiency of $5.5 billion in net increases in assets and in extended grants.[21] The area understated its estimated gross supply to all countries (including those within the area) by 43 per cent, and its receipts of repayments by 11 per cent. The deficiency in the supply includes the large French aid and investment flow to the dependencies whose exclusion from the French data is well known. But even if these amounts are excluded, the deficiency still amounts to 28 per cent of the gross supply, consisting of transactions whose omission is generally not apparent from the description of the data.

On the liability side a number of large adjustments in other records (mentioned below) made up the greater part of the over-all deficiency and the Continental OEEC's share was consequently less.[22]

[21] This amount consists of the net adjustments to changes in assets of $3,270 million in the line "Adjustments to reported accounts" in Table 2 plus $2,187 million net in unallocated changes in liabilities in excess of corresponding unallocated amounts on the asset side (contained in column 9 of Table 2), of which the Continental OEEC countries accounted for $2,793 million in adjustments and $1,864 million in unallocated amounts.

[22] Also, in this case, omitted receipts almost offset omitted repayments in the Continental accounts. The area only accounted, therefore, for less than 2 per cent of the over-all net deficiency of $3.3 billion, the latter amount consisting of the net $2,778 million in adjustments to reported accounts and of $483 in net unallocated amounts.

The area accounted for 15 per cent of the total deficiency in gross receipts (receipts of grants included), but for two-thirds of the total deficiency in repayments. It understated its estimated gross receipts of foreign capital and grants by 6 per cent, its repayments to all countries by 16 per cent. The deficiencies in the Continental OEEC reports occurred, however, mainly in the capital account, which made up only one-third of the Continent's gross receipts since two-thirds were in the form of U.S. grants. For receipts of foreign capital alone the deficiency amounts to 17 per cent.

The major part of the deficiencies in the reported data of all countries other than those of the Continental OEEC area is accounted for by a few large adjustments. Reinvested profits of the United Kingdom and Canada in the United States account for close to half of the deficiency in the gross supply of all other reporting countries; reinvested profits of the United States in the U.K. and Canada,[23] all direct investment in India, and the direct investment in the U.K. Overseas Territories (for the years for which it was not reported) account for three-fourths of the deficiency in gross receipts of all other reporting countries. The remainder of the deficiencies are scattered over all areas.

The deficiencies in reporting during the 1950–54 period, especially the understatement by the Continental OEEC area of its supply, are of particular interest if they are found to persist in the data for later years. Some insight into this question can be gained by reference to data for 1963 and 1964 in Smith's study of balance-of-payments asymmetries.[24] Smith's data are joint IMF-OECD data for OECD member countries, which include the French aid and investments flows to the former dependencies, and IMF data for the Rest of the World. The latter exclude, however, a number of underdeveloped countries, among them most of the former French dependencies and some Middle Eastern oil countries. The data are adjusted for the transactions of the International Institutions. Grants are combined with private dona-

[23] Canadian data for U.S. reinvested profits in Canada are available (although not included in the IMF account), but the magnitudes are unreliable because they include reclassifications. The adjustment in the Canadian data was made with U.S. figures. This amount accounts for 40 per cent of the deficiency in gross receipts of the countries outside the Continental OEEC area.

[24] John S. Smith, "Asymmetries and Errors in Reported Balance of Payments Statistics," *Staff Papers*, IMF, July 1967, p. 232, Table 6.

tions, for which reason no comparison can be made for this item.[25]

Smith aggregates all net transactions (1) between the OECD member countries,[26] (2) of the OECD countries with the Rest of the World, and (3) of the Rest of the World with the OECD countries. The net capital transactions between OECD members should, of course, come out to zero, but they show sizable net credits for both years, i.e., understatements of outflows ($3.6 billion and $1.5 billion, respectively). The OECD transactions with the Rest of the World show net outflows for both years. The Rest of the World's figures agree with the OECD figures to the extent that they show net inflows from that area, but the inflow falls short of the OECD outflow in 1963 (by $1.1 billion) and exceeds the latter in 1964 (by $.2 billion). The Rest of the World's net receipts are, however, understated by the incomplete country coverage and by omissions of reinvested profits in many cases, while these are included in the supply of not only the United States but also of the United Kingdom for these years, which together account for some 80 per cent of private investment. The Rest of the World's receipts, if they were complete, would probably exceed the OECD's outflow figures in both years.[27] Smith suggests, as one explanation of the net credits within the OECD area, the possible geographical misallocation of outflows between the OECD area and the Rest of the World. But in that case the outflow to the Rest of the World becomes smaller by the intra-OECD discrepancy, and would fall short considerably of the (incomplete) receipts of the Rest of the World in both years. Either way, some OECD members understate their outflows.

On the other hand, the figures are consistent with our findings. For 1950–54, the deficiency in the Continental OEEC supply includes considerable omissions of transactions within the later OECD area, namely of investments in, and loans and repayments to, other Conti-

[25] Smith's figures show underreporting of receipts of donations in both years, which is no doubt largely attributable to the incomplete country coverage. The adjustments to grants for 1950–54 consisted mainly of the then not reported French grants and of the transactions of nonreported accounts. Relatively few adjustments were made to reported accounts.

[26] The OECD consists of the sixteen former OEEC countries, the United States, Canada, Japan, and Spain.

[27] The Rest of the World's net figures also include, of course, any discrepancies between the data of the countries of the Rest of the World, but since the capital transactions between these countries are relatively small, the error is likely to be small also.

nental OEEC countries, the United States, and Canada, as well as omissions of transactions with the Rest of the World. At the same time there was no evidence in partner records during our period that the United States understated its outflow, and the British record was found to be reasonably complete, except for the partial omission of reinvested profits. But these have been included in the U.K. account since the late 1950's, both on the asset and on the liability side. It is, therefore, at least very likely that the missing outflow in Smith's figures is still attributable to an understatement of the Continental supply. The presumption that the statistics of the capital suppliers have better coverage of capital transactions than those of the under-developed countries is thus not borne out by these findings, as far as the Continental countries are concerned.

4

THE PATTERN OF CAPITAL
MOVEMENTS, 1950–54

We now proceed to the discussion of the pattern of capital flows during the period 1950–54. In the first four sections of this chapter the relative shares of the sources of the supply and the distribution of the various types of capital are considered. This discussion is based on Table 1 and on Appendix Tables B-I through B-VII, covering the individual types of capital. The next section discusses to what extent the capital supply of the United States, the United Kingdom, and the Continental countries of Group 1 was concentrated in the countries of the respective trade orientations. Differences in the composition of the capital supply of the U.K. and the Continent are also discussed. The last section of this chapter examines the distribution of government aid and private investment between the advanced and the underdeveloped countries.

An Over-All View

Total capital flows for the five-year period are shown in Table 1. As can be seen, the bulk of all capital was provided by the industrial countries (Group 1). If one eliminates the International Institutions as independent suppliers (since they were more or less intermediaries through which funds largely provided by Group 1 were channeled),[1] Group 1 supplied close to 90 per cent. For government capital and the major types of private long-term capital the percentages are even higher, from 92 to 96 per cent. But short-term movements flowing to Group 1 from the other groups raise the share of the latter to 10 per cent. These flows consisted mainly of increases in the dollar re-

[1] The European Institutions have been eliminated from Table 1 as independent suppliers (see the notes to Table 1).

serves and other liquid assets of all three of these groups and of a
$2 billion growth in the colonial sterling balances (Group 4).

The United States provided over half of all capital (55 per cent if
the institutions serving as intermediaries are excluded), the United
Kingdom approximately 9 per cent, and the Continent and Japan
over 25 per cent. In the share of the Continent and Japan short-term
movements again play a considerable part. These movements consisted of two flows: one within Group 1 to the U.S. in the form of
an increase in dollar reserves and other liquid assets of $3.5 billion
(of which Japan accounted for $.6 billion); the other consisting—
apart from EPU financing within Europe—mainly of export credits
and payments agreement balances extended to the other three groups.
The Continental credits, on the order of $1 billion, went mainly to
developing countries in Group 3, while Japan's ($200 million) went
to Far Eastern countries in Group 4. On the other hand, the United
States and the United Kingdom, as "key currency" countries, experi-
enced more moderate changes in their liquid currency assets; and
short-term credit extended by the U.S. was comparatively small, while
that of the U.K. decreased. The U.S. and U.K. were also the main
recipients of funds for repayments, redemptions, and repatriations,
which reduced their long-term capital outflows accordingly. The share
of the U.S. in the supply of grants and gross long-term capital and
that of the U.K. in the supply of private investment were thus considerably larger than the over-all percentages indicate [2]; the shares
of the Continent were correspondingly smaller. Japan provided virtually no long-term capital or grants during this period.

Aside from movements of reserve balances, the capital provided by
lenders outside Group 1 was supplied mainly by Group 2. It consisted of direct investment in all groups, the largest of which was,
however, Canadian investment in the United States. Another com-
ponent was the grants extended by Canada, Australia, and New
Zealand under the Colombo Plan to Asian countries in Group 4.
Among the Scandinavian countries, Finland paid reparations, and
Sweden extended a large loan, to Russia. But all these flows, other
than the Canadian investment, amounted to no more than one per

[2] The U.S. shares of grants and direct investment, the largest types of supply,
were 80 and 60 per cent, respectively; the U.K. supplied 21 per cent of direct
investment.

cent of the total. As lenders, except to Group 1, the other groups were therefore unimportant.

Virtually all of the capital provided to the rest of the world thus came from the industrial countries of Group 1. The capital supply of the United States was, however, the only one with global dimensions. Almost all countries received U.S. aid of some kind, and almost as many attracted American private investment. The capital supplied by the U.K. and the Continent was not only smaller, but also went to far fewer recipients.

The Distribution of Government Grants and Loans

Government grants and loans are shown in Appendix Tables B-I and B-Ia.[3] Government capital exceeded private investment in the total supply and in the supply to all groups except Group 2. The United States accounted for almost three-fourths of total government capital supplied. While U.S. government capital had many aspects and wide geographical distribution, the political forces of the time led to a high concentration of U.S. aid in several areas. The prime concern was still with European recovery, followed by mutual security and military build-up in the later part of the period. Close to 60 per cent of total U.S. aid consequently went to the industrial countries, Western Europe, and Japan (Group 1). A substantial part of U.S. grants and loans flowing to Group 2 was likewise in this category: recovery and mutual security aid to Scandinavia and loans for the production of strategic materials to Sterling Area countries.

While government aid for the development of backward countries had already been recognized as a necessary policy, the larger part of U.S. aid to the underdeveloped areas consisted also of aid for reconstruction and military emergencies. Of the countries of Group 3, those in Southeast Europe on the periphery of the Soviet bloc received the greater part of U.S. aid (Greece, Turkey, and Yugoslavia). Of the

[3] In Appendix Table B-I, grants and loans net of repayments are shown, while Appendix Table B-Ia gives grants and gross loans. In Appendix Table B-Ia grants and loans are classified by types and purposes. There are, of course, no sharp dividing lines between some of the categories. The distinction between aid to "strategic countries," where large aid was given in response to urgent cold war emergencies, and that to Iran and India ("development aid"), for instance, is perhaps one of degree only.

countries in Group 4, those in the Far East received the most (Korea, Taiwan, Philippines, and Indochina). What might be called "pure" development aid constituted only $2.1 billion, or 15 per cent of the total U.S. government capital supply of $14.7 billion during this period. The greater part of it, moreover, was in the form of loans, while most other U.S. aid was in the form of grants.[4]

U.S. aid to Europe may be said, however, to have done double duty. First, it gave rise to intra-European aid, which was directly induced by, and largely contingent upon, American aid. Second, it enabled the European countries to provide aid outside the OEEC region. The metropolitan powers supplied substantial aid to their dependencies. Aid received from the U.S. was far in excess of the aid extended by European countries, except in the case of France; even in this case, however, U.S. aid came close to the exceptionally large metropolitan aid. While the European aid also included emergency aid, like British aid to Malaya, it was largely development aid, and the combined European supply of this type of aid was absolutely larger than the corresponding American aid. Thus, although the pure development aid of the United States itself was small, the aid to Europe helped to generate aid to underdeveloped areas.

Relatively few independent countries received aid from European governments, apart from British-French participation in aid to Yugoslavia. What there was, moreover, consisted largely of contractual obligations, such as German and Italian reparations to Israel, Greece, and Yugoslavia. Virtually no European aid was extended to Europe's former colonies or spheres of influence in Asia and the Middle East. It was to these countries that the United States extended the larger part of its development aid, assuming to some extent responsibilities that had been vacated by the former colonial powers. The Greek-Turkish aid program is a celebrated example, but the pattern was widespread. Colombo Plan aid by Canada and Oceania also fulfilled this role.

On the other hand, the traditional American sphere of interest, Latin America, received only a small part of the development aid dispensed by the United States, and virtually all of it was in the form of loans, mainly Export-Import Bank loans. This Latin American aid, moreover, clearly contained the element of export promotion. Many

[4] See the recapitulation in Appendix Table B-Ib.

of the loan commitments dated back to the early 1940's before aid had become an official policy. Both in kinds of projects and in country distribution they were akin to the commercial loans of the period.[5] While total U.S. development aid was inversely related to the level of development, i.e., the absolute amounts increased from Group 2 downward,[6] much of the aid to Latin America went to the advanced countries of the region. All the Latin American countries in Groups 2 and 3 borrowed from the U.S., while only four of the eleven in Group 4 did so. This distribution is similar to that of private loans, which also covered the export of American equipment to the developing, rather than the underdeveloped, among these nations.

Aid by the International Institutions, IBRD loans, and UN grants constituted only 7 per cent of the total, of which IBRD loans accounted for two-thirds. While the first loans of the Bank had been for European reconstruction, during this period IBRD loans were made mainly for development, and the share of Group 1 was only 8 per cent. In the other groups the advanced countries were, however, the chief borrowers. The shares declined with the level of development, Groups 2, 3, and 4 receiving 44, 30, and 17 per cent, respectively, as did the ratio of the number of borrowers to member countries in each group.[7] The average size of the loans was also several times larger in Groups 2 and 3 than in Group 4. IBRD loans, the granting of which depends on the existence of well-planned, economically feasible projects, thus went mainly to more advanced countries which had a greater abundance of such projects. In view of this problem, the Bank had already instituted a policy of aiding underdeveloped countries, through technical missions, to plan feasible projects.[8] But the results of this policy were not reflected in the distribution until the later 1950's when close to half of the total amount of loans was made to Group 4. During the earlier period, the Bank provided, in effect, capital for expansion

---

[5] Over one-third of the Latin American aid total, a $300 million Export-Import Bank loan to Brazil, was in fact for the purpose of funding short-term debts to American exporters, i.e., for trade which had already taken place.

[6] See p. 79, below.

[7] In Group 2, 8 of 11 members borrowed; in Group 3, 5 out of 10; in Group 4, 10 out of 25. Moreover, the nonborrowers in Group 2 were Canada, which was not eligible since it had unlimited access to the market, and Sweden and Denmark, which were receiving American aid.

[8] For a discussion of the early policies of the IBRD, see Raymond F. Mikesell, *United States Economic Policy and International Relations,* New York, 1952, pp. 199–206.

of the overhead sector of the countries which also received, as we shall see, large manufacturing investment. The loans thus performed mainly the function of complementing private investment in those countries where it was concentrated rather than substituting for it in the least developed countries.

UN grants were of even less importance as aid to underdeveloped areas. Apart from Korean relief, they consisted, to a large degree, of refugee aid, mainly in Europe and the Arab countries. Since in the latter case the aid was in the form of imports for the refugee camps, it probably had little effect on the countries concerned (with the possible exception of Jordan where the refugees were somewhat more integrated with the economy). Economic and technical assistance was small. UN aid was thus more humanitarian than economic in nature, and the amount going to the underdeveloped countries themselves made up only a small fraction of their aid receipts.

The Distribution of Private Long-Term Capital

PORTFOLIO INVESTMENT

Portfolio investment, i.e., the underwriting of foreign securities in the financial centers ("Issues" in Appendix Table B-II), the chief form of international lending prior to the depression of the 1930's, did not regain its previous importance after the war. It accounted for only 20 per cent of the total private investment during this period, while direct investment made up 70 per cent and loans extended by the private sector, 10 per cent. The obstacles to the revival of portfolio investment lay in the widespread defaults of the interwar period and the restrictions on lending in European markets. To some degree the lack of demand by countries receiving large-scale aid also seems to have played a role, particularly in the case of the Western European countries. These countries borrowed only moderately in the Swiss market during this period, while they had floated some issues in New York before the Marshall Plan and did so more extensively after aid had ceased in the second half of the 1950's.

The underwriting of new issues was, therefore, highly selective. Apart from the issues of the IBRD (which was, of course, established because of the expected dearth of portfolio lending, and whose own borrowings accounted for more than one-fifth of total new issues), the issues of independent countries and those of the dependent territories must be distinguished. The latter were floated under favorable conditions in the metropolitan markets [9] and served largely to supplement aid (particularly in the British colonies and the Congo), but accounted for only one-fourth of the total (excluding IBRD issues).

Among independent countries, the advanced countries were the chief borrowers, with the countries of Group 2 more prominent than the industrial countries. Nine of the fifteen countries in this group were borrowers (three in two markets) compared to six in all other groups. Only two small new issues were floated by underdeveloped countries, Peru and Ceylon (the Panamanian issue represented refunding). Group 2, with 70 per cent of the total (excluding the IBRD), had the largest share in all of the three main markets where independent countries could or did borrow: the U.S., the U.K., and Switzerland. In the U.S., where Group 2 countries were the only borrowers, Canada and Israel accounted for most of the money raised. One may argue that these represent special cases, in that Canadian securities are not considered "foreign" by American investors,[10] and the Israeli issues had an emotional appeal. Yet the high economic level of Canada is, of course, responsible for the investors' attitudes, while the large inflow of skilled labor and managerial ability into Israel represents a condition that is absent in underdeveloped countries. The advanced economic level of these borrowers must be considered a precondition for their access to the market.

For balance-of-payments reasons, the British capital market was virtually restricted to the Sterling Area, but the domestic demands on the market curbed lending there also. Apart from the colonial and Rhodesian government issues, lending was confined to investment that would aid the balance of payments.[11] Under this criterion, mainly enterprises in the advanced sterling countries seem to have qualified,

[9] See, e.g., OEEC, *Sixth Report of the OEEC*, Paris, March 1955, Vol. II, p. 215.
[10] See Hal B. Lary and associates, *The United States in the World Economy*, U.S. Department of Commerce, 1943, p. 94; Ilse Mintz, *Deterioration in the Quality of Foreign Bonds Issued in the United States, 1920–1930*, New York, NBER, 1951, p. 10; and Paul Meek in *U.S. Private and Government Investment Abroad*, Raymond F. Mikesell, ed., Eugene, Ore., 1962, p. 241.
[11] *Midland Bank Review*, February 1952, p. 12; 1954, p. 12.

particularly the South African and Rhodesian mining companies with long-established markets.

With the exception of Switzerland, the Continental markets were generally closed to outsiders (except the dependencies) because of the domestic demand for reconstruction and balance-of-payments pressures.[12] While there were few restrictions in Switzerland until later,[13] the experience of defaults and unsatisfactory prewar debt agreements[14] also confined Swiss lending chiefly to advanced countries.

The outstanding securities that were bought (the positive entries for "Redemptions and Trading" in Appendix Table B-II) were also mainly those of the advanced countries, particularly those of the United States and Canada and, to a lesser extent, of Group 2 sterling countries.[15] Substantial purchases were also made of a few international blue chips, chiefly shares of the Shell group (in the Netherlands and the U.K.), British Petroleum (in the U.K.), and South African mining companies.[16]

While even among the advanced countries there were few whose securities were bought, among the underdeveloped there were fewer still, and most of the amounts were extremely small. Moreover, for the most part, these purchases do not seem to have been genuine portfolio transactions, but rather were connected with direct investment or were a by-product of other transactions. In the case of India, for instance, where the largest security purchases in Groups 3 and 4 were made, the amounts partly represent purchases of subsidiaries'

[12] The French and Italian markets were completely closed to outsiders, and the Dutch until 1954 (Paul Meek, "The Revival of International Capital Markets," *American Economic Review*, May 1960, p. 286; and UN, *The International Flow of Private Capital, 1956–1958*, New York, 1959, p. 65). The Dutch IBRD issue was floated in that year. There was possibly also a small issue by Surinam and one by the Belgian government, perhaps included in government loans.

[13] During the Suez crisis from 1956–58 the Swiss market was closed to foreign borrowers (see UN, *op. cit.*, p. 62); afterwards foreign access was rationed (see Charles P. Kindleberger, "European Economic Integration and the Development of a Single Financial Center for Long-Term Capital," *Weltwirtschaftliches Archiv*, Band 90, 1963, p. 200).

[14] See "Swiss Capital for Export," *Three Banks Review*, September 1951.

[15] Since the data for Redemptions and Trading in Table B-II are net totals for the five-year period, large redemptions or sales conceal substantial purchases in several cases, apparent from annual totals or other data, viz., Canada, where U.S. purchases were upward of $400 million; U.K. (by U.S., $26 million); and Australia and Rhodesia (by U.K., $23 and $11 million).

[16] See Paul Meek in *U.S. Private and Government Investment Abroad, op. cit.*, p. 247, and in *American Economic Review*, May 1960, p. 284.

obligations by foreign parent companies or by other buyers of the parent's nationality, and partly represent credit (by accepting shares) extended by foreign suppliers of machinery and equipment to Indian companies.[17] Acquisitions of securities are also the by-product of technical assistance when it is paid for in the shares of the assisted foreign enterprise.[18] Portfolio purchases in the ordinary sense were thus negligible in underdeveloped countries.

In brief, portfolio investment provided development capital only for the dependencies, not for the independent underdeveloped countries. How much access even the territories will have to the markets after independence remains to be seen.

DIRECT INVESTMENT

In contrast to portfolio lending, direct investment (Appendix Table B-III) was widely dispersed. The dispersion was greatest in the case of the United States, which accounted for 60 per cent of the total. While almost all countries received direct investment, it was the advanced countries (Groups 1 and 2) that attracted almost 70 per cent of the total.[19] Substantial investment was made in the industrial countries themselves, both by the U.S. in Europe, and by the latter in the U.S. There was also large Canadian investment in the U.S. and, to a smaller degree, Canadian investment in the United Kingdom. Intra-European investment was comparatively small, on the other hand, much smaller than trans-Atlantic investment by Europeans.

All the same, the direct investment capital inflow to Group 1 amounted to less than one-fourth of total direct investment. Group 2 again attracted the largest share, almost half of the total. Both the United States and the United Kingdom made their largest investments in the countries of this group—the U.S. in Canada, and the U.K. in the sterling countries, particularly in Australia and South Africa. It was characteristic of direct investment, moreover, that countries attracting large investments from the center of their trade-

17 See Reserve Bank of India, *Report on the Survey of India's Foreign Liabilities and Assets as on 31st December 1953*, Bombay, 1955, pp. 11–12, 84; and *Report . . . 31st December 1955*, Bombay, 1957, p. 11.

18 See Jack N. Behrman, "Promoting Free World Economic Development Through Direct Investment," *American Economic Review*, May 1960, p. 271.

19 The distribution of receipts by groups was: Group 1, 24.3 per cent; Group 2, 44.6 per cent; Group 3, 12.6 per cent; Group 4, 18.5 per cent (of which the Overseas Territories accounted for 9 per cent).

orientation often received additional direct investments from other sources, except in cases where the investment was primarily or exclusively in primary production. Thus, Canada attracted substantial investment from the U.K. and the Continent; the sterling countries from the U.S., the Continent, and each other. The large share of Group 2, therefore, was not only due to the very large U.S.-Canadian investment, but also to the fact that these advanced countries were generally attractive to investors.

In the underdeveloped areas, the largest U.S. investment was made in the more advanced Latin American countries of Group 3, exceeding the combined American investment in all other underdeveloped areas. These countries, especially Mexico, also received additional investments from other sources. The main European investment in the underdeveloped areas went to the overseas territories, the British investment in the dependencies being the largest. Few European investments were made in the independent underdeveloped countries other than the Latin American countries of Group 3. India was the only country to receive substantial British investment, accompanied by American and other investment. The independent countries of Group 4 received the smallest share of U.S. investment and very little direct investment from other countries. Direct investment was highly trade-oriented, moreover, so that Latin American and other U.S.-oriented countries obtained most of the American funds that did move to Group 4.

We defer a discussion of the industrial composition of direct investment until later. The question of the extent to which the investment was made in production for the market of the host country and the extent to which it consisted of investment in raw material production for export helps to explain the distribution between groups described above. This question will be treated below, where capital flows in relation to levels of development are considered in more detail.

PRIVATE LOANS

Loans by the private sector (shown in Appendix Table B-IV) were typically of intermediate-term maturities and largely offset by repayments. They were thus not a major vehicle for long-term capital transfers. The lenders were mainly American, Swiss, and other European banks (accounting for two-thirds of the total), and approximately two-thirds were made to governments or were guaranteed by the government of the borrower. Some large movements occurred between private concerns, chiefly of advanced countries, and a few loans to underdeveloped countries were extended by American and European firms supplying equipment and materials to, or operating in, these countries.

The loans were extended mainly to industrial or other advanced countries (72 per cent to Groups 1 and 2). In part these loans were connected with recovery aid (e.g., Export-Import Bank–guaranteed loans to Japan), and in part they replaced it, as aid diminished in the later years of the period. Among the underdeveloped countries only a few of the more advanced Latin American countries received major loans. The share of Group 4 amounted to only 5 per cent of the total.

REDEMPTIONS AND REPATRIATIONS

To what degree did return flows of private capital modify the distribution of the supply? Redemptions by, and foreign sales to, the residents of the debtor country of portfolio securities (the negative entries in Appendix Table B-II) [20] were largest for Group 2, which was also the largest recipient of private capital. While a number of underdeveloped countries made such payments, these were substantial only in the case of Brazil, and they were generally larger for the more advanced countries than for the least developed.

There were other return flows which came mainly from Groups 3 and 4, however. We have called them Extraordinary Repatriations (shown in Appendix Table B-V) because they took place largely as a result of political events or under political pressure.[21] Apart from special movements (such as the liquidation of Italian investment in settlement of reparations and the sale of German real estate by former refugees when the proceeds became transferable), they were repatriations largely of British capital from Latin America and, in the wake of independence, from former colonies. They consisted of com-

[20] Although a separation of redemptions from trading in Appendix Table B-II was not possible, the negative entries mostly seem to represent redemptions. In the case of the United States, which reports receipts of redemptions by area, these amount to over 80 per cent of the total.

[21] These transactions are reported in the host countries' records or other sources with indications that the entries were of this kind. They do not include ordinary repatriations of investment, which are netted out in the appropriate types of capital.

pensation payments for nationalizations and proceeds of sales, often to the host governments, of railroads, utilities, and other enterprises largely engaged in primary production. In the case of former colonies they included the liquidation and transfer of savings of departing personnel.[22]

The repatriation of ownership of railroads and utilities, mainly of British investment in Latin America, represented part of a process which started after the war and included the well-known sale of the Argentine railroads in 1947 to the Argentine Government for over £250 million. Many of these enterprises had become unprofitable, it is true, and the owners were willing to sell.[23] But in view of the continuing nationalizations of American and European utilities in Argentina, Brazil, and Colombia, for instance, sometimes by seizure, sometimes after a rate increase had been refused, one can assume that the British firms would have suffered the same fate.

In former dependencies, on the other hand, unfavorable investment climates led also to liquidations of previously profitable agricultural enterprises, particularly in Ceylon and to some degree in India,[24] while nationalizations occurred in some other countries.

Compared to the direct investment made during this period, the repatriations were small. They resulted, however, in net capital outflows from a number of the U.K.-oriented countries of Group 4 and reduced the net receipts of others substantially. The Latin American repatriations constituted, together with the large sterling bond redemptions by Brazil, a withdrawal of British capital in an area which had once been a major field of British investment.

Short-Term Capital Movements

In a number of countries short-term inflows supplemented long-term capital receipts. These movements consisted of cumulative short-term credits and, in some cases, of substantial drawings on currency reserves.

[22] This accounts for three-fourths of the outflow from India, and for the repatriation from Indonesia.

[23] See "British Investment in Latin America," *Three Banks Review*, June 1949.

[24] For the conditions that led to sales and breakups of efficient tea estates and rubber plantations in Ceylon, see IBRD, *The Economic Development of Ceylon*, 1953, pp. 24–25, 75 ff., 143, 516. Regarding the liquidation and sales of foreign enterprises in India, see Reserve Bank of India, *op. cit.*, 1955, pp. 19–20.

SHORT-TERM CREDITS

As far as short-term credit represents the customary financing of international trade or results from trade through the time element involved in transportation and payments procedures, it consists of temporary financing rather than capital movements. With increasing trade such short-term credit outstanding must necessarily increase, but normally for both the assets and liabilities of a country. Appendix Table B-VI shows, therefore, net inflows or outflows by groups of countries and for individual countries with major transactions in order to indicate where cumulative inflows occurred.[25]

Such cumulative credits were on the order of $1.3 billion. The lenders were mainly Germany and other Continental countries (approximately $900 million) and the United States and Japan ($200 million each). The credits consisted partly of formal export credits, mainly in the case of the Continent, and partly of "forced" credits in the form of payment arrears resulting from a lack of foreign exchange (mainly in the case of credits extended by the U.S.) and of payment agreements balances (Continent and Japan). The chief recipients of the U.S. and Continental credits were the more advanced underdeveloped countries in Latin America and Southern Europe (Group 3), where rapid development induced such movements. Brazil and Turkey were particularly heavy borrowers. The Japanese credits, covering largely textile exports, went to Far Eastern countries, three-fourths of the amount to Indonesia.[26] The Continental credits considerably exceeded all other capital provided by the Continent outside

[25] Appendix Table B-VI shows an over-all discrepancy, after all possible adjustments, between changes in assets and liabilities of $1.2 billion. From the pattern of discrepancies between areas in the matrix constructed on the basis of the IMF area system (mentioned above in the explanation of Type VI), it appeared that close to $1 billion of the total discrepancy represents credits provided, but not reported, by the Continent, well over half of this amount by Germany. This conclusion is supported by the error items in the German and other Continental countries' balances of payments and by other evidence (see e.g., UN, *The International Flow of Private Capital, 1956–1958, op. cit.*, pp. 71–75; Paul Meek, *American Economic Review*, May 1960, p. 287). We concluded that the Continent, instead of the net inflow of residual credit of $105 million shown in Appendix Table B-VI, had a net outflow on the order of $900 million to the other groups, mainly Group 3. For a fuller explanation, see Walther P. Michael, *op. cit.*, Appendix B, Matrix IX, pp. 354–366.

[26] Over-all, however, Japan was a net borrower, receiving credits from, or falling in arrears to, the U.S. ($60 million) and Europe ($90 million) in addition to net purchases from the Fund. Indonesia, on the other hand, made large repayments, mainly to the Netherlands.

the dependencies. To a large degree the Continental capital supply was, therefore, directly connected with export promotion.[27] In the case of Japan these credits were virtually the only capital provided.

RESERVES AND CORRESPONDENT ACCOUNTS

The increase in reserves and other liquid assets (Appendix Table B-VII) during this period occurred largely in the holdings of the advanced countries. The later Marshall Plan aid was used, as is well known, to build up reserves in both dollars and gold. But other advanced countries also showed substantial increases. While the majority of the underdeveloped countries also increased their reserves, the increase by group becomes smaller toward Group 4 (excluding dependencies), where it was negative, and where two-thirds of the decreases occurred. The large decreases consisted mainly of reductions in sterling balances, a good part of which had been accumulated during, and blocked after, World War II, but were then gradually released by the United Kingdom.[28] Sterling accumulations of the later 1940's, particularly by Continental countries, were then also decreased, so that there was a net reduction in the liabilities of the United Kingdom to independent countries of $.5 billion.[29] While the cases of over-all decreases in reserves are thus partly due to the withdrawals of excessive and involuntarily held sterling balances, balance-of-payments pressures led also to reductions in dollar reserves in Brazil and some other countries.[30]

The case of Ireland is of special interest because the larger part of external finance for its development was provided by the liquidation of Irish assets abroad. To the reduction in sterling balances (commercial bank assets in this case) must be added large sales of British securities by Irish investors. A comprehensive development program by

[27] See Paul Meek, *op. cit.*

[28] At the end of 1949, some $3.6 billion of World War II balances were still blocked, over half belonging to India, with Egypt and Pakistan accounting for another fourth. See "Who holds the Sterling Balances?", *The Banker*, May 1950, pp. 93 ff.

[29] The large increase in the colonial sterling balances represents a special case, which is discussed below.

[30] See also IMF, *International Reserves and Liquidity*, Washington, D.C., 1958. "In some countries, such as India, the reduction in reserves represented heavy spending on development" (p. 51); ". . . many non-industrialized countries have decreased their reserves. In some countries these decreases were planned and used to finance development" (p. 92).

the government caused extensive domestic investment by the private sector which was financed to a considerable degree by these repatriations of private capital, which had been invested in Britain during years of economic stagnation at home.[31] The Irish case suggests that other flight capital, such as the billions of dollars of Latin American capital supposedly placed in the United States and Switzerland,[32] may return if political and monetary stability is achieved in such countries.

Substantial inflows of short-term capital thus occurred in a number of cases, both in the form of credit and by drawing on reserve balances or other liquid assets. For some countries, movements in one form were cancelled out, however, by changes in the other (e.g., Colombia received large credits, but increased its reserves by a similar amount; the reduction in India's sterling balances was largely offset by a credit outflow). For others, the net addition to the long-term capital inflow was relatively small. It was only in Ireland (counting the portfolio repatriation), Brazil, Turkey, Pakistan, and Egypt that the additions were substantial. For the underdeveloped countries as a whole, these short-term movements increased the capital supply only moderately and mainly for the more advanced of these countries. For Group 3 it meant an addition of approximately 20 per cent to the long-term inflow of government and private capital, but for the independent countries of Group 4 the addition was less than 3 per cent.

The large increase in the sterling balances of the British Colonies, on the other hand, had a drastic effect since it offset by far British aid and investment in the territories, resulting in a net outflow from the Colonies to the United Kingdom of $600 million. The larger part of the balances represented the collaterals of currency boards and the funds of marketing boards and other official bodies, which were required by statute to be held, wholly or partly, in sterling securities.[33] While all the various territories increased their balances, three-fourths of the total was accounted for by West Africa, the Malayan region,

[31] See Chapter 3, footnote 9. The following amounts are involved: U.S. aid, $79 million (Appendix Table B-I); U.K. purchases of Irish bonds, $44 million (Appendix Table B-II); total foreign capital, $123 million; repatriation—sales of British securities, $131 million (Appendix Table B-II), repatriation—reserves, $29 million (Appendix Table B-VII), total Irish repatriation, $160 million.

[32] See, e.g., "Economic Development in South America," *JEC*, 87th Congress, 2nd Session, Washington, D.C., 1962, p. 1.

[33] See Ida Greaves, *The Colonial Sterling Balances*, Essays in International Finance, No. 20, Princeton, 1954, *passim*.

and Hong Kong. In Hong Kong the increase seems to have been due to large inflows of refugee capital and gold hoardings from mainland China.[34] In West Africa and Malaya the large sterling accumulations were due to high commodity prices and relatively low ratios of capital formation to gross product.[35] Particularly in West Africa exceptionally high cocoa prices caused large increases in sterling balances. These areas received also less aid and investment than East and Central Africa and the West Indies, which had higher capital formation ratios. This suggests that the receipt of external finance does lead to higher capital formation even though domestic resources may be available. Development plans have to be made in advance and depend on the funds which are expected to be available in grants and loans in the London market. Budget surpluses which are the result of commodity price rises, on the other hand, cannot be foreseen. It may not be possible to accelerate development as a result of such windfalls. Surpluses of marketing boards resulting from price increases must be held as a safeguard against future price declines. The resources which these colonial sterling balances represent were thus not available, or could not be utilized immediately, for the purposes which external financing was designed to accomplish.

Capital Flows and Trade Orientations

In this section we examine to what extent the aid and investment of the three centers, the United States, the United Kingdom, and the Continental OEEC countries, were concentrated in the countries whose trade relations were oriented towards them.[36] Some of the reasons for the distribution of capital which we observed will also be discussed.

The distribution of the long-term capital flows of the three main suppliers according to trade orientation is shown in Table 3. Since we are interested in the distribution of the capital supplied during this period, repayments have been eliminated from the table, i.e., loans included in government capital and private loans are shown gross,

[34] See the *New York Times,* November 8, 1959, p. 7.

[35] See OEEC, *Economic Development of Overseas Countries and Territories Associated with OEEC Member Countries,* Paris, August 1958, pp. 249–265, where the question of the sterling balances is treated in detail and which the discussion here follows in part. The capital formation data are for 1956, but they are unlikely to have changed much, and a time lag between receipt of funds and investment must be considered.

[36] For the classification of countries by trade orientations, see Appendix Table A.

TABLE 3

Distribution of Long-Term Capital of Group 1
Countries by Trade Orientation

	From					
	United States		United Kingdom		Continental OEEC	
To	Mil-lions of Dollars	Per Cent	Mil-lions of Dollars	Per Cent	Mil-lions of Dollars	Per Cent
U.S. and U.S.-oriented						
Government capital	3,226	22.5	107	10	139	4
Portfolio issues	1,175	99.0	–	–	19	4
Direct investment	4,936	72.0	625	25	678	53
Private loans	514	50.0	27	37	154	37
U.K. and U.K.-oriented						
Government capital	2,780	19.5	522	48.5	99	3
Portfolio issues	14	1.0	666	98.0	64	12
Direct investment	1,134	16.0	1,736	71.0	135	11
Private loans	212	20.0	46	63.0	17	4
Cont. OEEC and Cont. OEEC-oriented						
Government capital	8,218	58.0	447	41.5	3,057	93
Portfolio issues	–	–	14	2.0	428	84
Direct investment	795	12.0	98	4.0	460	36
Private loans	316	30.0	–	–	245	59

SOURCE: Matrix tables.

and redemptions and trading (Appendix Table B-II), consisting mainly of redemptions, and repatriations (Appendix Table B-V) have been excluded. For short-term credit the distribution could not be calculated.

The number of countries (including the countries of the centers themselves) in each of the three trade-orientations is approximately the same: twenty-seven in the U.S.-, twenty-six in the U.K.-, and twenty-nine in the Continental OEEC-oriented groups.[37] Thus, if the

[37] The British dependencies were counted as five units (Central Africa, West Africa, Western Hemisphere, Far East, Other); the French dependencies as three units (North Africa, Other Africa, Other); the Belgian, Dutch, Italian, and Portuguese dependencies as one unit each.

centers only supplied approximately one-third (or less) of a given type of capital to countries whose trade was oriented toward them, we would conclude that the distribution of this type of capital did not depend on the trade relationship of the recipient countries with the center. In Table 3 there are two of the twelve cases which fall in this category: the government capital of the U.S. and the direct investment of the Continent, where only 22.5 and 36 per cent, respectively, were supplied to their own trade orientations. In the other ten cases there was a definite concentration of the supply in the own trade orientations, ranging from approximately 50 to close to 100 per cent, which appears to indicate dependence on the trade orientation, although with considerable variation. In order to ascertain the reasons for the variation and to see how much meaning can be attached to the various percentages, we must examine the distribution of each type of capital more closely.

GOVERNMENT CAPITAL

The distribution of government capital may be assumed to depend on the political involvements of the donor country during the particular period. The small share of U.S.-oriented countries in American aid was, of course, the result of the global role which the United States had assumed. Recovery and mutual security aid to the Continental and Sterling OEEC countries was the major part, but American government capital went also to most other U.K.- and Continent-oriented countries. The share of the U.S.-oriented countries was thus less than one-fourth. A large part of this $3.2 billion, moreover, went to Far Eastern and other countries whose trade orientation toward the U.S. was, in considerable part, of recent origin and was, in fact, largely determined by this American aid, e.g., Korea, Taiwan, and Israel, where emergencies had arisen or new obligations had been assumed. Latin America, on the other hand, the traditional sphere of U.S. commercial interests, received only one-fourth of this amount.[38] Thus the global commitments which the United States assumed after World War II had the result that only a small share of American aid went to U.S.-oriented countries, particularly those in Latin America with the older trade ties to the U.S.

In the United Kingdom and the Continental OEEC countries, which

[38] See also the discussion on pp. 48–49 above.

had long-standing political and commercial ties with the colonial territories, the shares of countries oriented toward them were higher.
In the case of the U.K. it was still less than half of the total, but in
the case of the Continent it was over 90 per cent. British aid to the
territories and to independent Sterling Area countries was relatively
small. British grants and loans under the OEEC arrangements (IEPA
and EPU grants and consolidation loans of payment arrears), aid to
Yugoslavia, a loan to a Canadian corporation for the production of
strategic materials, and various settlements with U.S.- and Continent-
oriented countries accounted, therefore, for somewhat more than half
of the U.K. total. Continental governments also had obligations to
countries outside their own trade orientation (e.g., the German compensation payments to U.S.-oriented Israel). But the fact that grants
and loans under OEEC arrangements were mainly extended between
Continental countries and the large size of the French colonial aid
(close to $2 billion) resulted in the high concentration of Continental
government capital in their own trade-orientation group.

PORTFOLIO ISSUES

Portfolio lending showed a very high concentration in the trade
orientations of all three centers. There seems to be no prima facie
reason for this, however, since security flotations, largely funds raised
by governments, do not necessarily finance trade directly and may not
even be spent abroad. If there are no other constraints, interest rate
differentials presumably determine the market in which a borrower
floats an issue. In the past, the main financial centers, New York and
London, had been global lenders. In the last peak period of portfolio
lending, the decade of the 1920's, some fifty countries borrowed in
New York.[39] The explanation of this high concentration during the
1950–54 period lies in the factors curbing portfolio lending mentioned
previously, namely, the experience of defaults during the Depression,
which resulted in very selective lending, and the restrictions of the
European markets because of balance-of-payments pressures. The issues
floated in the U.S. were thus virtually only those of the two special
cases, Canada and Israel, while borrowing in the U.K. and in Continental metropolitan countries was mainly or entirely confined to their

---

[39] Ralph A. Young, *Handbook on American Underwriting of Foreign Securities,*
U.S. Department of Commerce, Washington, D.C., pp. 11, 20, 75–137.

respective currency areas. The trade orientations underlie, of course, the currency areas, but it was the confinement of lending to the latter which was the determining factor. Switzerland alone resembled the markets of the past by lending to countries in all three trade orientations, although on a modest scale.

DIRECT INVESTMENT

Direct investment has a closer connection with trade than portfolio investment, since machinery and equipment for subsidiaries and branches are often supplied directly by the parent companies, investment in finance and trade are frequently connected with imports and exports, and investment in primary production is usually made for the purpose of supplying agricultural and mineral products to the center. Consequently we do find a fairly high concentration of this type of investment by the United States and the United Kingdom, the main suppliers, in countries of their respective trade orientations, although not for the smaller Continental investment. The high percentage in the case of the United States is of particular significance because, in contrast to the other lenders, the U.S. spread its investments very widely and the pattern is, therefore, less influenced by random factors. An industrial breakdown is also available for U.S. investment,[40] which makes it possible to ascertain the extent of the concentration by industrial sectors. In every sector over half of the investment was made in the U.S.-oriented countries, although with considerable variation in the percentages. The concentration was highest in primary production (agriculture, 100, petroleum exploration and extraction, 90, mining, 86 per cent) and in utilities and transportation (99 per cent). It was over 70 per cent in services (trade, 72, and other, 79 per cent), and it was least in manufacturing (61 per cent) and petroleum refining and distribution (51 per cent). This

[40] The *Survey of Current Business* provides breakdowns into seven sectors. Petroleum, which is reported as one sector, was divided into (1) exploration and extraction, and (2) refining and distribution, with information contained in the *Oil and Gas Journal*. This was done in order to separate (1) investment mainly for export from (2) investment for consumption in the host country. For major oil-producing countries the petroleum investment was considered to be entirely in exploration and extraction, since refineries in these countries mainly serve export.

In some cases where several sectors are combined in *Survey of Current Business* tables, the divisions were estimated from regional totals or other evidence. For references see Appendix B, Statistical Sources for Appendix Tables B-I to B-VII (United States).

variation is due to the fact that the investments in the different sectors were also dependent on the level of development of the countries in which they were made. In order to examine the relative importance of trade orientation and levels of development in the distribution, it is best to exclude Canada (Group 2, U.S.-oriented), which accounted for 42 per cent of total U.S. direct investment and for almost half of the investment in primary production. Its proximity to the United States was, one may assume, a more important factor than its level of development in attracting large investments in primary production. If Canada is excluded, still as much as 52 per cent of U.S. direct investment went to U.S.-oriented countries, but in manufacturing and petroleum refining and distribution the percentages fall to 37 and 30 per cent, respectively. Table 4 throws light on the relative importance of trade orientation and level of development in the distribution of the investment in each sector by relating the concentration of the investment in U.S.-oriented countries to that in Groups 3 and 4. As the table shows, investment in industries that went mainly to underdeveloped countries was highly trade-oriented. This is particu-

TABLE 4

Partial Distribution of U.S. Direct Investment, by Sectors, Between Trade Orientation and Economic Levels of Host Countries, 1950–54

(*per cent*)

	Percentage of U.S. Direct Investment Going to	
	U.S.-Oriented Countries	Group 3 and 4 Countries
Agriculture	100	100
Mining	73	73
Petroleum exploration and extraction	79	99
Utilities and transportation	99	99
Trade	58	64
Other	56	38
Manufacturing	37	37
Petroleum refining and distribution	30	29

NOTE: Excluding Canada.

larly true of investment in the production of primary goods, which generally constitute the main exports of underdeveloped countries to the center, and of investment in utilities and transportation.[41] Investment in manufacturing and in petroleum refining and distribution, on the other hand, was attracted to the markets of the high-income countries and was, therefore, more related to the advanced level of the countries in which it was made. Manufacturing investment is often made to "jump over tariff walls," while oil refining may use crude oil originating in third countries. These industries are, therefore, not especially associated with trade with the center.

In the Trade, Other (services), and Manufacturing sectors, substantial investment was made in the U.S.-oriented Latin American countries of Group 3. In other words, the investment in these sectors made in the underdeveloped countries was mainly in the more advanced among them, and the dependence seems to have been as much on the more advanced economic levels as on the trade orientation of the countries. This is particularly true of Manufacturing where Group 4 alone received only 4 per cent of the total investment (excluding Canada), indicating the strong dependence of this investment on more advanced levels of development.

For the other two centers, the United Kingdom and the Continent, the relation of the composition of investment to trade orientation and levels of development seems to have been similar.[42] Investment in primary production was very largely made in countries of their own trade orientation—chiefly in the dependencies, which received the major part of European investment in the underdeveloped areas. Investment in secondary and tertiary sectors, on the other hand, was chiefly in Groups 1 and 2 and was less dependent on trade orientation. The bulk of British investment outside the Sterling Area went to the U.S. and Canada and was mainly in manufacturing and services, including large insurance investments in the U.S. In the case of the Continent relatively large investments in secondary and tertiary industries outside countries of their own trade orientation made up, in fact,

[41] Utility and transportation investments as well as agricultural investments were small, however, accounting together for only 3 per cent of U.S. investment. Such investments were encountering increasing animosity in the host countries.

[42] Breakdowns by sectors are not available in these cases, but the approximate composition of the major part of the investments could be ascertained from partner data or other evidence.

the greater part of the total. It was mainly the sizable investment in the United States by two smaller countries, the Netherlands (in the petroleum refining and distribution sector) and Switzerland (in manufacturing), which accounted for the low share (37 per cent) of the Continent and Continent-oriented countries themselves. The distribution by sectors of the U.K.'s and the Continent's investment is, therefore, not inconsistent with the findings in the case of the United States. We shall come back to the distribution of investment by industries in relation to economic levels in the next section.

PRIVATE LOANS

The percentages of private loans indicate dependence on trade orientation in all three cases. The United Kingdom, where the concentration was largest (63 per cent in the U.K.-oriented countries), extended few loans, however, and the high percentage may not be very meaningful since these loans went entirely to one country, South Africa. The United States, the largest lender, showed the lowest concentration (50 per cent in the U.S.-oriented countries), while that of the Continent in the Continent-oriented countries was 59 per cent. The distribution of the loans of these two lenders by countries was quite similar, however. A large part of the American loans outside the own trade orientation was extended to Europe. These loans were chiefly for general balance-of-payments purposes (i.e., hard currency loans) and they served to supplement or replace the diminishing aid (as mentioned above). The Swiss loans, which made up the greater part of the Continental loans *within* the own trade orientation, were of the same nature and went roughly to the same countries. On the other hand, the American loans *within* the own trade orientation went mainly to developing countries in Latin America, but the Continental loans extended *outside* the own trade orientation also went chiefly to these same countries. These latter loans were more directly connected with exports, often financing equipment for development projects. In the case of the Continental loans, they resulted, therefore, from the efforts of the European countries to re-establish their export trade and conquer new markets. Although one would expect these export loans to follow the trade orientation this was not the case. Thus, the relation of private loans to trade orientation seems to be rather weak and not clearly established.

The apparently high dependence of capital flows on trade orientation observed in Table 3 is, therefore, somewhat misleading with regard to private capital. The high concentration of portfolio lending in the respective trade orientations was largely due to special circumstances. For direct investment the relationship varied by industrial sector: Investment in primary production and utilities—which predominated in underdeveloped countries—was highly trade-oriented; investment in manufacturing and oil refining and distribution, which was attracted mainly by advanced countries, showed little dependence; and investment in trade and other services, which also went largely to more advanced countries, showed a relatively weak dependence on trade orientation. For private loans no firm conclusions could be drawn.

SOME OTHER ASPECTS OF THE PATTERN

There are some other aspects of the pattern of capital flows during this period which deserve comment, namely, the capital supply of the United Kingdom and the Continent to the underdeveloped areas and differences between them. In contrast to the United States, the European countries extended aid to few underdeveloped countries outside the dependencies. The early fifties were, of course, still a period of reconstruction in Europe. The demands of the home economies continued to be great. In Britain, the center of the Sterling Area, it seemed particularly imperative to minimize drains on reserves and to guard against inflation lest the pound be endangered. British government aid was not only small in comparison to the large French aid, but also in relation to its private capital supply. The countries of Asia and the Middle East were very largely in the Sterling Area. A number of them were Commonwealth members, and others were within the British sphere of influence. Yet few of them received British aid. The British considered releases of the sterling balances that had been accumulated by a number of countries during the war as a kind of aid, since the resulting "unrequited exports" put a strain on the British economy. But such releases were of some substance only in the cases of Egypt and Pakistan during this period. The demands of home investment and defense, and the domestic demand for consumer durables, seem to have also prevented an increase in export credits. Such credits, mainly finance capital goods and British exports of these goods, generally did not rise, and sometimes declined, during this period.[43] The extraordinary increase in export credits which took place in the case of the Continental countries thus did not occur in Britain.

However, having been historically the chief capital market of the world, Britain relied mainly on private capital to aid underdeveloped countries.[44] Thus, colonial aid was supplemented with London bond issues of colonial governments. The British also felt an obligation to give the Commonwealth members access to the market,[45] but few government issues resulted; among underdeveloped countries only Ceylon qualified for, or chose to float, a small issue. British delegations to the Colombo Plan conferences pointed to the investment being made in India as evidence of the contribution of British private investment.[46] The British investment in India was, however, the exception rather than the rule. British direct investment abroad was indeed considerable, but it went in large part to advanced countries. In the underdeveloped areas it was chiefly made in the territories which were still under British control and which also received most of the aid.[47] Thus, British investment cannot be said to have taken the place of aid in the former empire.

In Latin America, where British investment had been large, there was also a retreat rather than an expansion of British capital. And colonial aid and investment were more than offset by the capital inflow into the U.K. in the form of colonial sterling balances. As a result of these uphill flows, the United Kingdom's net capital supply to the underdeveloped areas as a whole was, in fact, negligible.

Continental aid and investment in the underdeveloped areas were concentrated in the dependencies. By far the largest part of this flow during the period under review consisted of $2 billion in French

[43] See Peter B. Kenen, *British Monetary Policy and the Balance of Payments, 1951–1957*, Cambridge, 1960, pp. 24–26.

[44] Cmnd. 237, July 1957, *The United Kingdom's Role in Commonwealth Development;* see also A. R. Conan, *Capital Imports into Sterling Countries*, London, 1960, pp. 98–100.

[45] See *Midland Bank Review*, February 1954, p. 12, and *Colombo Plan, 3rd Annual Report*, Ottawa, 1954, p. 103.

[46] Cmd. 9622, October 1955, "The Colombo Plan," U.K. section.

[47] It may well be that the lack of adequate data on British investment led to a misinterpretation of its direction.

colonial aid. The explanation of this large aid to the dependencies—on an even larger scale in subsequent years—is to be found in the French policy to induce the territories to maintain close political, cultural, and economic relations with the mother country after independence. As M. Pompidou has put it more recently: ". . . for us Frenchmen it is somehow a need to defend the French tongue . . . [against] . . . a strengthening of the position of the English language" (to which multilateral aid would lead).[48]

The bulk of the Continent's capital supply to the independent underdeveloped countries consisted of the $1 billion in export credits, which went, however, mainly to Group 3, the more advanced among these countries. These countries received, as mentioned previously, similar loans and credits from the United States, while the other aid they obtained consisted largely of IBRD loans. Since the "capacity to repay" is presumably greater for more advanced countries than for the least developed,[49] there is some justification for supplying aid through loans rather than grants to these countries. Nevertheless, the extent to which this kind of finance was resorted to has a number of disadvantages. Short-term credits are at best a haphazard way of financing development, since planning requires knowledge of the extent to which external finance will be available.[50] And the cumulative short-term credits and the bunching of intermediate-term and long-term loans have caused continuous balance-of-payments problems in a number of countries.

Capital Flows and Levels of Development

PRIVATE CAPITAL

In the previous sections we saw that the larger part of private capital went to the advanced countries. The receipts of government and private long-term capital by countries and country groups are shown in Table 5 both in absolute amounts and per capita. Of the total supply of private capital of $12.9 billion, net, only 28 per cent

---

[48] Quoted by Goran Ohlin, *Foreign Aid Policies Reconsidered*, OECD, Paris, 1966, p. 32; see also pp. 27–33 for a discussion of the controversy over foreign aid in France.

[49] See P. N. Rosenstein-Rodan, "International Aid for Underdeveloped Countries," *Review of Economics and Statistics*, May 1961, p. 109.

[50] *Ibid.*, p. 144.

TABLE 5

Receipts of Government and Private Long-Term Capital, Net of Repayments,
Total Aggregative and Per Capita Amounts, 1950–54

	Total Receipts (millions of U.S. dollars)			Receipts Per Capita (U.S. dollars)		
	Total	Govern-ment	Pri-vate	Total	Govern-ment	Pri-vate
Total	28,897	16,015	12,882			
GROUP 1	9,521	6,578	2,943	21.05	14.55	6.50
US	1,792	–	1,792	11.80	–	11.80
UK	1,742	1,189	553	34.65	23.65	11.00
Continent	5,301	4,872	429	31.70	29.15	2.55
Japan	686	517	169	8.30	6.25	2.05
GROUP 2	8,146	1,799	6,347	89.00	19.65	69.35
Canada	3,915	74	3,841	285.75	5.40	280.35
Israel	781	478	303	600.80	367.70	233.10
Chile	143	22	121	23.45	3.60	19.85
UK-oriented	2,534	584	1,950	78.95	18.20	60.75
Iceland	38	37	1	265.50	258.50	7.00
Ireland	123	79	44	41.05	26.40	14.65
Australia	859	190	669	104.80	23.20	81.60
New Zealand	138	−1	139	72.60	−.55	73.15
Rhodesia	394	86	308	61.55	13.40	48.15
S. Africa	982	193	789	78.50	15.40	63.10
Cont.-oriented	773	641	132	20.20	16.75	3.45
Denmark	114	165	−51	26.55	38.40	−11.85
Norway	336	299	37	101.80	90.60	11.20
Sweden	86	66	20	12.30	9.45	2.85
Finland	−26	−24	−2	−6.50	−6.00	−.50
Argentina	172	91	81	10.00	5.30	4.70
Uruguay	(91)	44	(47)	(36.40)	17.60	(18.80)
GROUP 3	3,766	2,545	1,221	20.55	13.90	6.65
US-oriented	1,921	683	1,238	19.10	6.80	12.30
Brazil	818	456	362	15.70	8.75	6.95
Colombia	157	56	101	13.90	4.95	8.95
Cuba	154	14	140	28.55	2.60	25.95
Mexico	394	149	245	15.30	5.80	9.50
Panama	49	5	44	61.25	6.25	55.00
Venezuela	349	3	346	64.60	.55	64.05

(*continued*)

TABLE 5 (*continued*)

	Total Receipts (millions of U.S. dollars)			Receipts Per Capita (U.S. dollars)		
	Total	Govern-ment	Pri-vate	Total	Govern-ment	Pri-vate
GROUP 3 (continued)						
Cont.-oriented	1,845	1,862	−17	22.40	22.60	−.20
Greece	811	803	8	106.70	105.65	1.05
Portugal	83	65	18	9.90	7.75	2.15
Turkey	311	301	10	14.90	14.40	.50
Spain	63	77	−14	2.25	2.75	−.50
Lebanon	5	7	−2	3.85	5.40	−1.55
Yugoslavia	572	609	−37	35.30	37.60	−2.30
GROUP 4	7,464	5,093	2,371	8.40	5.75	2.65
US-oriented	2,120	1,516	604	25.25	18.05	7.20
Latin America	320	105	215	11.45	3.75	7.70
Costa Rica	7	4	3	8.75	5.00	3.75
Dom. Rep.	31	1	30	14.80	.50	14.30
El Salvador	12	13	−1	6.30	6.85	−.55
Guatemala	3	1	2	1.05	.35	.70
Haiti	28	13	15	8.75	4.05	4.70
Honduras	42	3	39	30.00	2.15	27.85
Nicaragua	14	6	8	12.75	5.45	7.30
Bolivia	37	34	3	12.35	11.35	1.00
Ecuador	32	13	19	10.00	4.05	5.95
Peru	114	17	97	13.40	2.00	11.40
Philippines	330	255	75	16.55	12.80	3.75
S. Korea	746	746	–	35.20	35.20	–
Taiwan	359	342	17	47.85	45.60	2.25
Liberia	46	9	37	57.50	11.25	46.25
S. Arabia	262	2	260	43.85	.50	43.35
Ryukyus	57	57	–	81.45	81.45	–
UK-oriented	2,512	1,354	1,158	3.60	1.95	1.65
Independents	1,126	991	135	1.80	1.60	.20
Burma	−30	−12	−18	−1.60	−.65	−.95
Ceylon	−5	12	−17	−.65	1.50	−2.15
India	445	326	119	1.25	.90	.35
Pakistan	195	169	26	2.60	2.25	.35
Iraq	59	9	50	12.30	1.90	10.40
Jordan	148	148	–	113.85	113.85	–
Libya [a]	43	43	–	43.00	43.00	–

(*continued*)

TABLE 5 (*concluded*)

	Total Receipts (millions of U.S. dollars)			Receipts Per Capita (U.S. dollars)		
	Total	Govern- ment	Pri- vate	Total	Govern- ment	Pri- vate
GROUP 4 (continued)						
UK-oriented						
Independents						
Afghanistan	24	24	–	2.40	2.40	–
Indonesia	62	91	−29	.80	1.20	.40
Iran	137	137	–	7.20	7.20	–
Nepal	1	1	–	.15	.15	–
Thailand	36	39	−3	1.95	2.10	−.15
Ethiopia	28	12	16	1.65	.70	.95
Sudan	−17	−8	−9	−1.95	−.90	−1.05
UK Overseas Terr.	1,386	363	1,023	18.00	4.70	13.30
Cont.-oriented	2,832	2,223	609	27.25	21.40	5.85
Independents	20	27	−7	.80	1.05	−.25
Egypt	1	10	−9	.05	.50	−.45
Syria	9	8	1	2.80	2.50	.30
Paraguay	10	9	1	7.15	6.45	.70
Cont. Overseas						
Terr.	2,812	2,196	616	35.85	28.00	7.85
French	2,444	1,995	449	49.00	40.00	9.00
Belgian	223	79	144	14.40	5.10	9.30
Dutch	59	43	16	53.65	39.10	14.55
Ital. Somali [a]	51	51	–	42.50	42.50	–
Portuguese	35	28	7	3.20	2.55	.65

NOTE: Excluding Soviet Bloc, Indochina, and Australian New Guinea. Parentheses indicate the figures are questionable. They are reported as "estimates," which are probably overstated; the identified private capital cancels out approximately.

SOURCE: Appendix Tables B-I through B-V; population data (1950), U.N. *Demographic Yearbook*, 1955, pp. 115 ff., and 1963, Table 4.

[a] Includes budgetary aid.

went to the underdeveloped areas (Groups 3 and 4). Among the advanced countries it was those of Group 2, however, that received the main share, close to one half of the total. Both major types, portfolio and direct investment, favored Group 2, as did both major suppliers of private investment, the United States and the United Kingdom. The underdeveloped areas as a whole account, however, for two-thirds of the world population (excluding communist countries), and Group 4 alone for over half, while Group 2 makes up only 6 per cent. Per capita receipts of private capital declined, therefore, sharply from Group 2 downward, i.e., the lower the per capita income of the group, the smaller was the inflow of private investment per capita (see last column of Table 5).

We pointed out previously the reasons why portfolio investment has by and large avoided the underdeveloped countries since the Depression and the war. Presumably, however, direct investment, the dominant form of private capital, is especially suited to the needs of the underdeveloped countries because technological knowledge and managerial skill are provided with the capital. Yet, the underdeveloped areas attracted only a small share of the total. An explanation for the relative sparseness of foreign investment in underdeveloped areas was provided by the late Ragnar Nurkse, who gave two reasons. First, underdeveloped countries do not attract investment for the domestic market because their low per capita incomes yield insufficient aggregate demand. The investment in these areas is, therefore, frequently in raw material production for export—an often observed phenomenon. But, Nurkse continued, the markets for raw materials are not expanding to the extent that they did in the nineteenth century, and synthetic substitutes have diminished the demand, curbing this form of direct investment also.[51]

We have already discussed the industrial composition of direct investment in the context of trade orientation. We found that (if Canada is excluded) U.S. investment in primary production was mainly made in underdeveloped countries, but that the more advanced among them, those in Group 3, also attracted substantial investment in manufacturing and services. By groups, the distribution of U.S. direct investment between primary production and other sectors is shown in Table 6.

On a per capita basis [52] the largest investments were made in ad-

[51] Ragnar Nurkse, *Problems of Capital Formation in Underdeveloped Countries,* New York, 1953, pp. 24–31, 82–89; see also UN, *International Capital Movements in the Inter-War Period,* 1949, p. 32.

[52] Per capita receipts of direct investment alone were, in U.S. dollars:

Group 1	6.20	*Group 3*	8.70
		US-oriented	13.60
Group 2	55.70	Cont.-oriented	1.10
US-oriented	160.60		
UK-oriented	44.20	*Group 4*	2.40
Cont.-oriented	9.40	US-oriented	7.40
		UK-oriented	1.70
		Cont.-oriented	3.10

TABLE 6

Distribution of U.S. Direct Investment Between Primary
and All Other Sectors, 1950–54

(*per cent*)

Country Group	Primary Production	All Other [a]	Not Specified
Group 1	–	100	–
Group 2	36	64	–
Group 2 ex. Canada	21	79	–
Group 3	27	70	3
Group 4	70	28	2

NOTE: The evidence for the other investor countries suggests that the composition was similar, viz.: primary production was nil or negligible in Group 1, constituted the smaller part in Groups 2 and 3 (and a smaller proportion in Group 3 than in Group 2), but accounted for two-thirds or more of the investment in Group 4 (see Walther P. Michael, "International Capital Movements, The Experience of the Early Fifties (1950–1954)," Ph.D. dissertation, Columbia University, 1965, pp. 163–172).

SOURCE: See footnote 40 in text.

[a] Including petroleum refining and distribution.

vanced countries with expanding markets, particularly those of Group 2 and to a smaller degree in the intermediate Latin American countries of Group 3. But, while investments in the manufacturing and service sectors of the countries in these groups were generally large, substantial investments in the primary sector were also made in several of these countries. Where investments of the latter type were large in these countries they were accompanied by still substantial investments in other sectors. Among the countries where both kinds were combined were particularly Canada, South Africa, Cuba, and Venezuela. On the other hand, investment was relatively smaller in those groups of countries where it was only made in nonprimary sectors, as in the Continent-oriented countries of Group 3, or mainly in the primary sector, as in Group 4. Group 1 also falls in this category, in that only nonprimary investment was made, but here more limited opportunities for foreign investment during this period were presumably the main reason for the lower per capita figure. The Scandinavian countries (in Continent-oriented Group 2) are on the Group 1 level with the exception of Norway where investment in shipping was large.

The first part of Nurkse's explanation seems, therefore, to be borne out: investment for the domestic market declined with per capita incomes.[53] In the majority of the underdeveloped countries, those in Group 4 with the lowest incomes, it was generally small and scattered. As far as the flow of capital into primary production is concerned, however, it is not so much that this investment was small but that it went to a considerable degree to more advanced countries. The American mining and oil extraction investment in Canada alone, in excess of $1 billion, exceeded the whole U.S. investment in Group 4.

A further factor accounting for the low receipts of some areas was an "unfavorable investment climate" or the existence of military emergencies in a number of countries. Particularly in several U.K.-oriented countries of Group 4 whose receipts were among the lowest, and where raw material investment had previously been important, no investment was made or repatriations occurred.[54]

This pattern of private investment was not unlike that of the half century before World War I. Data on capital movements during that period are far from complete, particularly with regard to the underdeveloped countries of today. But there seems little doubt that the largest investments were made in the "areas of recent settlement." [55] These are the countries that are included in our Group 2, except that the largest capital importer of that period, the United States, has replaced Britain as the largest supplier. As several writers have pointed out,[56] the capital flows to these countries complemented enormous immigration of skilled labor, providing the overhead capital which opened up the new lands and gave their products access to the world market.

This description does not fit the conditions in the early 1950's except in one case, the newcomer Israel, with its large immigration. Although we noted special motivations in the supply of portfolio capital to Israel, that country does present some similarities to the

[53] See also Peter B. Kenen, *Giant Among Nations,* 1962 edition, p. 128–129.

[54] For example, Iran under the Mossadegh regime, and Indonesia, where small investments were offset by disinvestments; see also Appendix Table B-V.

[55] See Ragnar Nurkse, "International Investment Today in the Light of Nineteenth Century Experience," *Economic Journal,* December 1954, pp. 744–758; see also Douglass C. North in *U.S. Private and Government Investment Abroad, op. cit.,* pp. 31 ff.

[56] Nurkse, *ibid.;* North, *ibid.;* A. K. Cairncross, *Home and Foreign Investment, 1870–1913,* Cambridge, 1953, p. 209.

areas of recent settlement of the nineteenth century. Its receipt of private capital per capita greatly exceeded those of all other countries except Canada, and if one includes government aid, its per capita receipts of $600 for the five years were more than twice even those of Canada. But immigration does not provide the explanation for the continued concentration of private investment in the other countries of this group. Having achieved a modern infrastructure and generally high living standards, these countries now attracted investment mainly in manufacturing and services, although in some cases substantial raw material investment continued or was begun. This situation was not wholly unique to Group 2. It also prevailed in the more advanced Latin American countries in Group 3, especially Brazil, Colombia, and Mexico.

Conditions in the underdeveloped areas, however, are very different from those in the developing countries of the past. Consequently, in the majority of the underdeveloped countries private capital provided neither for social overhead development nor for industrial diversification. Colonial administrations had access to the metropolitan capital markets, it is true, but these were restricted by the heavy demand placed upon them by reconstruction at home. The territories involved accounted also for only 14 per cent of the population of Group 4. In a few cases oil companies made substantial investments in refineries for the domestic market, namely in India and the Philippines, but in the latter case the inducement was mainly the granting of exploration franchises which were contingent upon the refinery. Otherwise private capital was attracted mostly by primary production in these areas, investment in secondary and tertiary industries being generally small and scattered. This conforms also to the pattern of the past.[57]

The disadvantages of this kind of investment for underdeveloped countries have often been pointed out. It is said to create or perpetuate "dual economies," in which the efficient export sector, utilizing foreign technology and often foreign personnel, may not induce further development in the indigenous subsistence sector.[58] Moreover, the establishments are usually much larger than in other industries. During the

[57] Ragnar Nurkse, *Problems of Capital Formation, op. cit.*, p. 84; see also North, *op. cit.*, p. 34.

[58] H. W. Singer, "The Distribution of Gains between Investing and Borrowing Countries," *American Economic Review*, May 1950, pp. 475–477; see also Nurkse, *Problems of Capital Formation, op. cit.*, and P. N. Rosenstein-Rodan, *op. cit.*, p. 110.

period 1951–57, for instance, primary investment accounted for 49 per cent of the *value* of new establishments founded by U.S. parent companies, but for only 19 per cent of their *number*.[59] The diffusion of the effect of the investment on the economy is thus likely to be much smaller than for other industries. The very scale of the operations requires equipment that cannot be produced in these countries and has to be imported.[60] On the other hand, in countries where modern technology and scientific methods have not penetrated at all, this kind of investment may provide new social services, such as education and medical services, as in the well-known case of Aramco in Saudi Arabia. Furthermore, royalties and tax receipts provide the government with important sources of development funds, and export proceeds supply needed foreign exchange. While raw material investment for export is, therefore, certainly not without benefit, it is not likely to have as great and direct an effect on the development of the host country as does investment for the domestic market.[61]

Although the share of the underdeveloped areas in private capital was relatively small, per capita receipts varied considerably within groups. Such variation is attributable, of course, to a number of factors, but it is accentuated by raw material investment, since large amounts of such investment are frequently made in countries with relatively small populations. The sixteen U.S.-oriented countries in Group 4, for instance, had the highest per capita receipts of direct investment in that group ($7.40 as given in footnote 52 above); but if Peru and Saudi Arabia with large mining and petroleum investment are excluded, the figure falls to $3.90.

GOVERNMENT CAPITAL AND PRIVATE INVESTMENT

In view of the fact that private investment was largely attracted to advanced countries, how did the distribution of government capital compare to that of private capital? Due to the massive European recovery aid, the share of Group 1 was, of course, the largest, 41 per cent of the total of $16,015 million shown in Table 5. But this was

[59] U.S. Department of Commerce, *U.S. Business Investments in Foreign Countries,* Washington, D.C., 1960, p. 100. The petroleum sector includes refining and distribution; if only exploration and extraction were included, the phenomenon would probably be more pronounced.

[60] Kenen, *op. cit.,* p. 118.

[61] See also Nurkse, *Problems of Capital Formation, op. cit.,* pp. 24–25 and 84.

peculiar to this period. For the three capital importing groups the shares increased downward, from 11 to 16 to 32 per cent for Groups 2, 3, and 4, respectively. This pattern was true of each major donor-lender, the U.S., the U.K.,[62] and the Continent. In the latter two cases, however, the distribution was influenced by reparations and other contractual payments, while their development aid went mainly to the dependencies where their private investment in the under-developed areas was also concentrated. The distribution is more inter-esting in the case of the United States, which supplied the larger part of both aid and investment, and whose capital was globally dispersed. In this case the distribution of government aid was inversely related to that of private capital in the three groups, the shares of private capital decreasing, and those of government aid increasing with the declining level of development, as seen in the text table.

	Government Aid (per cent)	Private Capital (per cent)
Group 2	21	68
Group 3	35	18
Group 4	44	14
Total	100	100

While these figures include emergency aid, which is influenced by factors exogenous to economic level, development aid showed a simi-lar distribution (24, 33, and 42 per cent). The available supply of U.S. aid was thus distributed so as to somewhat offset the inverse relation-ship between receipts of private capital and level of development.

Returning to Table 5, we find, however, that per capita receipts of government capital, like those of private capital, declined with the level of development from Group 2 downward. On a per capita basis, Group 2 had the highest receipts not only of private capital, but also of official capital. (If the U.S. population is excluded, Group 1 showed the highest per capita aid receipts.) While Group 2 includes most of the countries which were least eligible for government aid (e.g., Canada and the sterling countries), IBRD loans and govern-ment loans for the supply of strategic materials raised the per capita

[62] For the U.K., Group 2 aid was larger than that extended to Group 3; but the former includes a consolidation loan, i.e., not new capital.

receipts of official capital above those of most underdeveloped countries. In Groups 3 and 4, moreover, all aid receipts over $10 per capita were cases of aid for reconstruction, political or military emergencies and famine relief, or aid to dependencies or countries under Allied administration. The countries and territories involved accounted for only 17 per cent of the population of Groups 3 and 4 (excluding the Soviet Bloc). The more or less pure development aid to independent countries resulted in the lowest per capita receipts. Moreover, these declined with the level of development. Thus, on a per capita basis, government aid did not compensate the underdeveloped areas for their small share of private capital.

The question whether the aid to the underdeveloped areas during this period was inadequate can be answered, however, only with reference to the "absorptive capacity" for capital of these countries. Unfortunately, there is as yet no generally accepted method of calculating the amounts which these countries could productively employ. The estimates of capital requirements which have been made are generally projections for the 1960's and 1970's. Some of these are based on parameters of past economic performance of individual countries with assumptions about possible growth rates limited by absorptive capacity. Others are estimates of the projected "foreign exchange gap." [63] The estimates vary widely in the magnitude of the required aid. A comparison with even the lowest of these estimates, those by Rosenstein-Rodan,[64] which assume extremely moderate growth rates for most countries, would suggest that the aid actually extended during 1950–54 was grossly inadequate. It amounted to 30 per cent of the estimated requirements of the underdeveloped countries as a whole. But since aid was highly concentrated, for most countries the discrepancies between aid and requirements were much larger than this average, while in the few countries with very high receipts the requirements were exceeded. In the countries with the lowest per capita incomes, the U.K.- and Continent-oriented independent countries of Group 4, the aid receipts came to approximately 10 per cent of requirements estimated by Rosenstein-Rodan.

[63] See Goran Ohlin, *op. cit.,* pp. 76–80, for a comparison of the various estimates.
[64] Rosenstein-Rodan, *op. cit.;* these estimates are also the most suitable for comparison because they were made for individual countries; for the comparison see Walther P. Michael, *op. cit.,* pp. 266–270.

THE FEASIBILITY OF
CONSTRUCTING CAPITAL FLOW
ACCOUNTS FOR LATER PERIODS

The pattern of capital movements described above covers an early part of the postwar period. While some aspects of this pattern, particularly the concentration of U.S. aid in Europe, were peculiar to this period, the distribution of private investment and aid among the capital importing groups is not. How this distribution works out for later years, after aid to Europe had ceased and European recovery had been accomplished, must remain for further study.

A continuation of this study would very likely encounter problems similar to those for the early 1950's, although improvements in the reported data have taken place. The staff of the Balance of Payments Division of the Fund has, of course, exerted steady efforts in this respect, and new information has become available in many cases. The U.K. balance of payments, which included only net figures for private capital, distinguishes, from 1958 on, assets and liabilities, and direct and other investment. A country breakdown of direct investment (including reinvested profits) is also available beginning with 1958, although there are some gaps in the coverage.[1] While the procedure in this case obviously will be simplified, the British account still will have to be supplemented with partner data and other sources, even from 1958 on. The records of the continental countries seem to have improved also, as spot checks of balance-of-payments reports reveal, and as is also indicated by the tables of aid and investment flows to the underdeveloped countries in the OECD studies, which are based on member countries' reports.[2] Private investment seems generally better covered and identified by type. Regional distributions by cur-

---

[1] H. M. Stationery Office, *Board of Trade Journal*, 6 October 1961, pp. 715–720.
[2] See, e.g., OECD, *The Flow of Financial Resources to Less-Developed Countries. 1956–1963*, Paris, 1964.

rency areas, which were of very limited use, have been replaced by more meaningful ones. While these improvements have come only gradually (Sweden, for instance, omits all direct investment until 1962), the identification of the Continental transactions will be made easier for later years than for the early 1950's.

On the other hand, there is the evidence, discussed above, which seemed to indicate that the Continental countries continued to understate their outflows in 1963 and 1964. The procedure will, therefore, still have to rely heavily on partner data and other sources to identify the capital flows of the European suppliers and supplement their data not only for the years directly following 1954 but probably for later years as well. There are always details of information available in the balance-of-payments statements, investment censuses, or other sources of some countries that make it possible to identify transactions and to fill gaps in other records. The publications of the OECD and the UN will also be very useful, particularly regarding the flow of official capital.

One problem in any attempt to reconstruct capital flows for recent periods is the length of time which elapses before the reported data are firm. At present each of the Fund's Yearbooks carries revisions of the data for the four years preceding the latest one covered. There is, therefore, always a lag of five years at the time of publication of the most recent data. In the process of this study substantial revisions were encountered in a number of important accounts. Very large revisions in the U.S. direct investment figures, particularly of the data for foreign investment in the U.S., did not appear until 1963.

It is hoped that the data can be further improved, especially those of the Continental countries. It would also be very helpful if for the transactions of these countries more detailed breakdowns could be provided, particularly of private capital, of the kind which the United States supplies, and which are also now available for the United Kingdom. It should be possible to improve balance-of-payments data to the point where one can construct integrated accounts of world capital transactions on an annual basis. Such accounts would be of obvious value to students of international trade and economic development. It is hoped that this study will contribute in some measure toward this end.

Appendix A

AREA SYSTEM

APPENDIX TABLE A

Area System According to Economic Level and Trade Orientation
in Early 1950's

	US and US-Oriented		UK and UK-Oriented		Continental OEEC and OEEC-Oriented	
	Country	Data	Country	Data	Country	Data
GROUP 1	US	1,870	UK	780	Aus	370
		12 & 2		5 & 4		19 & 1
		7 & 2		6 & 4		16
	Jpn	190			Bel	800
		33 & 2				11 & 6 (1947)
		26 & 3				8 & 5
					Fr	740
						20
						17 [a]
					Ger	510
						12 & n.a.
						12 & n.a.
					Ity	310
						35
						32
					Nth	500
						17 & 2 (1947)
						13 & 2
					Swi	(1) 1,010
						(2) 15 [b]

GROUP 2

Country			
Can	1,310	19 & 2	7 & 2
Isr	470	12 [a]	12
Chi	360	29 & 6 [b]	15 & 6
Ice	(1) 780	(2) 41 (1940)	
Ire	410	36 [b]	31
Asl	950	17 & 2 (1947)	17 (1939) [a] & n.a.
NZ	1,000	20 (1945)	24 & 1
RFd	[c]		
SAf	(1) 300		
Nonwhites	(2) 44 & 12 (1946) [b]		
Whites	(2) 14 & 6 (1951) [b]		
	(3) 18 & 13		
Swd	950	19	13 [a]
Den	750	19	21
Nor	740	25 & 1	15 & 1
Fin	670	34	25
Arg	460	26 (1947)	16 & 1
Uru	n.a.		

(continued)

APPENDIX TABLE A (continued)

	US and US-Oriented		UK and UK-Oriented		Continental OEEC and OEEC-Oriented	
	Coun-try	Data	Coun-try	Data	Coun-try	Data
GROUP 3	Bra	230			Gr	220
		56 & 3				44 [b]
		29 & n.a.				34
	Col	250			Por	200
		53 & 1.5 [b]				44 & 1 [b]
		43 & 2				31 & 1
	Cub	(1) 310			Tur	210
		(2) 41 (1953) [b]				76
						49 & 1
	Mex	220			Sp	(2) 47 & 2 [b]
		58 & 1 [b,d]				(3) 41 & 2
		20 & 4				
	Pan	220			Leb	(1) 260
		49 [b]				(3) 20
		34				
	Ven	(1) 540			Yug	(2) 54 (1953) [b]
		(2) 40 & 3 [b]			SBI (USSR)	(2) 58 (1939) [a]

GROUP 4

CR	(2) 54[b]	Bur	50		Par	140	
	(3) 45		69 & 1[e]			53[b]	
			47 & 2			44	
Dom	(1) 160	Cey	110		Egy	120	
	(2) 56[b]		44 (1946)			61 (1947)	
			55[a]			44	
ElS	(2) 62[b]						
	(3) 53						
Gua	160	Ind	60		Syr	n.a.	
	78 (1940)		69				
	46		51 & 1		COT		
Hai	(2) 73[b]	Pak	70		Alg	(2) 75	
	(3) 74		70		Mor	(2) 67[a]	
			60		Con	(2) 85[a] & n.a.	
						(3) 30 & 20	
Hon	150	Irq	(1) (100)				
	73 (1940)						
	56 & 1	Jor	n.a.				
Nic	(2) 67 & 1[b]	Lby	n.a.				
	(3) 41 & 6	Ins	(1) (50)				
Bol	(60)	Java	(2) 65[e]				
	42 & 7[b]	Other	(2) 78[e]				
	56[a] & n.a.		(3) 56 & 2				
		Tha	80				

(continued)

APPENDIX TABLE A (*concluded*)

	US and US-Oriented		UK and UK-Oriented		Continental OEEC and OEEC-Oriented	
	Country	Data	Country	Data	Country	Data
GROUP 4 (cont.)	Ecu	150 47 & 5 [b] 39 & 2		76 (1947) 57 & 2		
			Irn	(1) (100)		
	Per	120 54 & 2 (1940) 37 & 11	Eth	(1) (50)		
			Sud	n.a.		
	Phi	150 60 41 & 1	Afg	n.a.		
			Nep	n.a.		
	Tai	(3) 37 & 1	UKOT			
	SK	(1) 70 (3) 53 & 1	Jam	(1) 180 (3) 31		
	SAr	n.a.	BrG	(3) 27 & 10		

Lib		n.a.
BrH	(3)	38
Cyp	(2)	47 (1946) & n.a.
	(3)	29 & 13
Mal & Sin		310
		50 & 2 (1947)
		38 & 8
H K	(3)	4
G C	(3)	40 & 9
Nig	(3)	69
Ken	(1)	60
	(3)	44
Uga	(1)	50
SR	(3)	23 & 10
Nya	(3)	56 (1948) [a]

[a] Kuznets' data.
[b] U.N. Stat. Yearbook 1957 data.
[c] Rhodesian Fed. (1) 100

NR & Nya (2) 8 & 28 (Europeans only) [b]
SR   (2) 11 & 4 (Europeans only) [b]
NR   (3) 10 & 63 (1947–53) [a]

[d] Includes women in agriculture.
[e] 1930 or 1931.
n.a. = not available.

STATISTICAL NOTES FOR APPENDIX TABLE A

NOTE: For each country, the information on the first line is per capita income (in U.S. dollars) for 1952–54. For a few countries not covered by the 1952–54 data, the 1949 figures were used (these appear in parentheses).

The first figure in the second line indicates the percentage of the adult male labor force in agriculture. The second figure in the second line indicates the percentage of the labor force in mining. The first figure in the third line is the percentage of total product contributed by agriculture. The second figure is the percentage contribution by mining to total product, which is shown where significant. If information was not available for all three lines, the type of data available is indicated by the line number in parentheses. Unless otherwise indicated, the figures in the second and third lines are those for 1950, or within two years of 1950. If another year was used, it is indicated within parentheses.

See the statistical notes to Appendix B for abbreviations.

SOURCE: Line 1—United Nations, Series E, No. 4, *Per Capita National Product of Fifty-five Countries, 1952–1954* (averages). The more extensive but less reliable data for 1949 come from UN, Series E, No. 1, *National and Per Capita Incomes, Seventy Countries, 1949*.

Line 2—Colin Clark data from the *Conditions of Economic Progress*, 2nd ed., 1957, p. 510, Table III. Where only data before 1945 were available, the percentage was based on UN data, *Statistical Yearbook 1957*, Table 6, p. 50 ff., by excluding females in agriculture. These data are for 1950 or within a close range, but the coverage by ages is uneven; children are included in a number of cases. In a few cases, where neither data were available, Kuznets' data were used, from *Industrial Distribution of National Product and Labor Force*, Appendix Table III. These include both women and children.

Line 3—Agriculture—Calculated from UN, Series H, Nos. 8, 9, and 10, *Industrial Origin of Gross (Net) Domestic Product*, for 1950. The results were checked, however, against the Kuznets' data (*op. cit.*, Appendix Table I) which are calculated for a longer period, usually 1948–54. In 22 cases the result is the same, in most others it differs by one or two points. The largest difference is in the case of Egypt where the Kuznets' figure is 9 per cent lower (35 per cent); this is partly due to a rise in the government sector. The Kuznets' data were used where UN data were unavailable. Mining—The mining sector was also shown where significant. The comparison of labor force and product percentages, although giving a very rough result, indicates that mining, unlike agriculture, is at least of average, and often above average, productivity for the country.

Appendix B

CAPITAL FLOW TABLES

Appendix Tables B-I to B-VII cover the individual types of capital flows by countries of origin and destination (with the exception of Appendix Table B-VI, as explained below). For the sake of simplicity, the countries for which the transactions constitute changes in assets are called "lenders" (although some of the types consist partly of equity capital); and the countries for which the transactions constitute changes in liabilities are called "borrowers." In Appendix Tables B-I to B-V the lenders (and donors of grants) appear in the box heads, or in the columns where groups of countries are combined under one column heading, the borrowers (and recipients of grants) in the stubs. In Appendix Table B-VII, Reserves and Correspondent Accounts, the holders of foreign currencies – the lenders – appear in the stub. Appendix Table B-VI shows only the net short-term credit inflows and outflows by country for reasons explained in the text.

The figures represent the total flows during the five years, 1950–54.

Some reported transactions were excluded from the tables. A few small transactions covering life insurance funds and real estate transactions were excluded from the table since they could not be classified under any of the major types. Also excluded were certain "bookkeeping" transactions which are not relevant for the purpose of this study. The latter consist of cancellations of contingent liabilities of Belgium and Indonesia; Australian and New Zealand transactions with U.K.-Dominion Wool Disposal Ltd., which are in the nature of merchandise consignments; Indian receipts of annuities from the U.K. and offsetting payments of pensions and amortization to the U.K.; U.S. vestings and divestings of alien property; and the assumption by Germany of $1 billion of American grant-aid as a liability.

Conversions of one type of capital into another, such as the fundings of short-term credits, are included, however, in the respective types of capital (that is, as if there were a repayment of the short-term item and a new flow of long-term capital).

Appendix Tables B-I to B-VII follow. Notes for each table are at the end of the individual table. Statistical notes and a list of abbreviations for all the tables follow Appendix Table B-VII.

APPENDIX TABLE B-I

Government Grants and Net Loans, Five-Year Totals, 1950–54

(millions of dollars)

Borrowers (recipients)		Lenders (donors)										
			Group 1						Other Groups		Eur. Inst. IEPA, EPU	Int. Inst. UN, IBRD
		Total	Total	US	UK	France	OthCOEEC & Jpn	2, 3, 4	Can-ada	Other		
Total aid		17,995	16,043	12,649	732	2,024	638	−93	−223	130	735	1,310
Grants		15,729	14,249	11,963	896	707	683 [a]	334	71	263 [b]	700	446
Loans, net		2,266	1,794	686	−164	1,317	−45	−427	−294	−133	35	864
Group 1	Total aid	6,578	6,585	6,950	−270	−11	−84	−358	−242	−116	342	9
	Grants	8,040	7,677	7,647	1		29	21	17	4	342	
	Loans	−1,462	−1,092	−697	−271	−11	−113	−379	−259	−120		9
UK	Grants	1,717	1,711	1,711				6	6			
	Loans	−528	−250	−239		−6	Bel −3 / Ita −2	−278	−197	Por −4 / Cey −7 / Ind −19 / Jor −3 / UKOT −48		
Aus	Grants	523	395	395	−3						128	
	Loans	−16	−16	−12		−1	Uni 3 [a]					
Bel	Grants	264	264	261			Nth 26	−15	−17	Con 2		37
	Loans	−10	−32	−53			Uni −5					

Country	Type	(1)	(2)	(3)	(4)	(5)	Breakdown A	(6)	(7)	Breakdown B	(8)	(9)
Fr	Grants	2,006	1,960	1,936			Ita 24[a], Bel −3, Swi −58, Nth −5			Den −1, Swe −9, Sp −3, Swe 2, Una 1, Den −2	46	−1
	Loans	−496	−437	−209	−162			−58	−45			
Ger	Grants	1,126	1,058	1,057	1			3			65	
	Loans	−100	−98	−24	−42	−1	Bel −1, Swi −30	−2				
Ita	Grants	961	961	961						Arg −10, Una 1		20
	Loans	−58	−68	−58		−1						
Nth	Grants	604	500	498			Swi −9, Uni 2[a]	−10, 1			103	
	Loans	−259	−185	−121	−64			−16		Swe −12, Ant −4		−58
Swi	Loans	−2	−2			−2						
ECCS	Loans	59	59	59								
Uni OEEC	Grants	293	282	282			Ger −6, Swi −17	11	11			
	Loans	−23	−23									
Jpn	Grants	546	546	546								
	Loans	−29	−40	−40								
Group 2	Total aid	1,799	1,309	1,036	150	−1	124	−46	−8	−38	119	11, 417
	Grants	883	768	589	44		135	6		6	109	
	Loans	916	541	447	106	−1	−11	−52	−8	−44	10	417
Can	Loans	74	74	8	66							
Chi	Grants	5	5	5								
	Loans	17	24	24								
Isr	Grants	366	366	217	18[c]		Ger 131[a]	−18		Arg −18		11
	Loans	112	116	116								
Ice	Grants	26	22	22				−4		Jor −4	4	
	Loans	11	4	3	1			1		Den 1		6

(continued)

APPENDIX TABLE B-I (continued)

Borrowers (recipients)	Total	Group 1 Total	US	UK	France	OthCOEEC & Jpn	2, 3, 4	Can-ada	Other	Eur. Inst. IEPA, EPU	Int. Inst. UN, IBRD
Group 2 (cont.)											
Ire Grants	14	14	14								
Ire Loans	65	65	65								
Asl Grants	2	2									
Asl Loans	188	10	4	6		Ger & Jpn	2[a]				178
NZ Loans	−1	−1	−1								
RFd Grants	13	13		13							
RFd Loans	73	35	31	4							38
SAf Loans	193	91	91								102
Den Grants	138	127	127								
Den Loans	27	34	14	29		Swi −5 Uni −4	3 −7		Swe 3 Swe −7	8	
Nor Grants	257	157	155			Uni 2[a]	3		Swe 3	97	
Nor Loans	42	−7	−5			Bel −4 Uni 2	14	−8	Swe 22	10	25
Swe Grants	48	48	48								
Swe Loans	18	18	18								
Fin Loans	−24	−13	−13				−38		Swe 1 Arg −35 Bra −2 Col −1 USSR −1		27

Lenders (donors)

Country	Item	1	2	3	4	5	6	7	8	9	10
Arg	Loans	14	14	1		−1					
	Grants										
Uru	Loans	30									
Group 3	Total aid	2,658	1,925	1,721	36	22	146	162	180	274	297
	Grants	1,794	1,407	1,158	67	27	155	127	127	249	11
	Loans	864	518	563	−31	−5	−9	35	53	25	286
Bra	Grants	33	33	10				−18			
	Loans	423	314	314	23[a]			−18			109
Col	Grants	3	3	3							
	Loans	53	15	15			−2				40
Cub	Grants	1	1	1				−2			
	Loans	13	13	13							
Mex	Grants	30	30	30							
	Loans	119	59	59							60
Pan	Grants	5	5	5							
	Loans	1	1	1							
Ven	Grants	2	2	2							
Gr	Grants	837	655	554	−12		Uni 101[a]			179	3[e]
	Loans	−34	−34	−22							
Tur	Grants	252	192	192	−29	−2	Ger −10	3	Irq 3; Yug −1; SBl −5	57	28
	Loans	49	2	43				−6		25	
Por	Grants	29	16	13	3[a]					13	
	Loans	36	36	36							
Sp	Grants	13	13	13							
	Loans	64	64	65							
Yug	Grants	459	452	330	41	−1	Uni 54[a]				7[e]
	Loans	150	101	53	47	27	Nth 1				49
Leb	Grants	10	9	9		−2					1[f]
	Loans	−3	−3	−1							

(continued)

APPENDIX TABLE B-I (*continued*)

Borrowers (recipients)		Total	Lenders (donors)								Eur. Inst. IEPA, EPU	Int. Inst. UN, IBRD
			Group 1					Other Groups				
			Total	US	UK	France	OthCOEEC & Jpn	2, 3, 4	Can-ada	Other		
Group 3 (cont.)												
USSR	Grants	102	-22	-22				124		Fin 124[b]		
	Loans	60	-17		-17			77	-3	Swe 80		
OSBl	Grants	19	19	19								
	Loans	-68	-34	-14	-20			-34	-13	Den -4 Nor -3 Swe -12 Bra -2		
Group 4	Total aid	5,231	4,884	2,334	437	1,987	126	46	32	14		301
	Grants	3,343	3,117	1,961	405	653	98	77	41	36		149
	Loans	1,888	1,767	373	32	1,334	28	-31	-9	-22		152
CR	Grants	5	5	5								
	Loans	-1	-1	-1								
Dom	Grants	1	1	1								
EIS	Grants	2	2	2								
	Loans	11	-1	-1								12
Gua	Grants	1	1	1								
Hai	Grants	5	5	5								
	Loans	8	8	8								
Hon	Grants	3	3	3								
Nic	Grants	3	3	3								
	Loans	3	-2	-2								5

Recipient	Type	(1)	(2)	(3)	Jpn	Other donor	Other donor	Named donors	Total
Bol	Grants	19	19	19					
Bol	Loans	15	15	15					
Ecu	Grants	5	4	4		1		Gua 1	
Ecu	Loans	8	8	8					
Per	Grants	8	8	8					4
Per	Loans	9	13	13					
Phi	Grants	245	245	245		−8		Arg −8	
Phi	Loans	10	10	10					
Ryl	Grants	57	57	57					
SK	Grants	750	672	672		3		Tha 3	75[g]
SK	Loans	−4	−4	−4					
Tai	Grants	356	356	348					
Tai	Loans	−14	−14	−14					
Lib	Grants	4	4	4					
Lib	Loans	5	5	5					
SAr	Grants	2	2	2					
Bur	Grants	19	19	19	8[a]				
Bur	Loans	−31	−13	−2		−18		Ind −18	
Cey	Loans	11		−11		11	6	Asl 3 / NZ 2	1
Cey	Grants	1							
Ind	Loans	1				29	17	Asl 11 / NZ 1	27
Ind	Grants	111	82	82					
Pak	Loans	215	188	188		30	18	Asl 10 / NZ 2	25
Pak	Grants	123	93	93					
Nep	Loans	46	21	15			6		
Nep	Grants	1	1	1					
Irq	Grants	4	4	4					6
Irq	Loans	5	−1	−1					
Jor	Grants	136	77	13		64			
Jor	Loans	12	12	12		12			59[f]

(continued)

APPENDIX TABLE B-I (*concluded*)

			Group 1						Other Groups		Eur. Inst. IEPA, EPU	Int. Inst. UN, IBRD
Borrowers (recipients)		Total	Total	US	UK	France	OthCOEEC & Jpn	2, 3, 4	Can-ada	Other		
Group 4 (cont.)												
Lby	Grants	43	42	7	26	9						1
UKOT	Total aid	363	363	20	343							
EAf & Ade	Grants	70	70		70							
EAf & Ade	Loans	11	11	3	8							
WAf	Grants	50	50		50							
Mal & FE	Grants	105	105		105							
Mal & FE	Loans	23	23		23							
BWI	Grants	53	53		53							
BWI	Loans	16	16	16								
Oth & Una	Grants	35	35	1	34							
Oth & Una	Loans	1	1	1								
Afg	Grants	23	23	23								
Ins	Grants	59	57	53			Nth 4	2		Asl 1 / NZ 1		
Ins	Loans	32	47	55			Nth −8	−15	−9	Asl −6		
Irn	Grants	133	133	130	3[d]							
Irn	Loans	4	4	4								
Tha	Grants	22	22	22								
Tha	Loans	−5	−5	−4	−1							
Eth	Grants	8	8	5			Ita 3[a]					22
Eth	Loans	−1	−1	−1								
Sud	Grants	−4	−1	−1				−2		Swe −2		
Sud	Loans	−8	−4		−4			−4		Egy −4		7

Par	Grants	4	4	4						2
	Loans	5	−3	−3						1 e
Egy	Grants	12	11	8		Ita 3 a		6	Bra 6	
	Loans	−2	−2	−2						
Syr	Grants	14	1	1						13 f
	Loans	−6						−6	Leb −10	
									SAr 4	41
								17	17	40
COT	Total aid	2,334	2,276	182	1,978	Bel 116		17		
BelC	Loans	79	39	17		Nth 22				1
NthOT	Grants	29	29			Nth 29				
	Loans	14	14			Nth 14				
FrOT	Grants	782	782	138	644					
	Loans	1,351	1,350	16	1,334					
ItS	Grants	51	51			Ita 51				
PorOT	Grants	1						1	Por 1	
	Loans	27	11	11				16	Por 16	
EurI										
EPU	Grants	428	418	238	151	Bel 29		10	Swe 10	
IEPA	Grants	438	380		27	Aus 3		58	Den 5	
					115	Bel 135			Nor 6	
						Ger 54			Swe 29	
						Ita 29			Por 8	
						Nth 17			Tur 10	
EPU	Loans	30	30			Bel 30				
BIS	Loans	30	30			Swi 30				
UN	Grants	446	426	348	78			20	Asl 5	
							13	Pak 1	
								Tha 1	
Una & rounding	Grants	357	56	22	35 h	−1		15	Nor 14	286 i
								Tha 1	

NOTES TO APPENDIX TABLE B-I.

^a Reparations: Total grants in this column (683) include reparation payments of 330 by Germany (163), Italy (159), and Japan (8), which are approximately equal to total receipts; the division between receipts from Germany and Italy cannot be made in all cases.

^b Finnish reparations to USSR (124) included in total grants in this column (263).

^c Palestine settlement (see also footnote h).

^d Revaluations of sterling balances, held at the time of the 1949 devaluation, reported by UK (total 42); allocation between Brazil and Uruguay estimated, may include small amounts of Chile and Paraguay; Portugal may include Belgium (country allocation based on *The Banker*, "Who holds the Sterling Balances?", May 1950, pp. 93 ff.).

^e UNICEF.

^f UNRWA.

^g UNKRA.

^h Unallocated Sterling Area; the Palestine settlement (18) to Israel was assumed to be included by UK in the Sterling Area figure. If this is not the case the unallocated amount is 53.

ⁱ Miscellaneous, possibly not completely disbursed.

NOTE: See the List of Abbreviations at the end of Appendix B. A minus sign indicates net repayments.

Discrepancies (after adjustments, if any) of partners' figures from those entered in the table:

Grants. Although a number of entries were reported by only one side or were identified by partner country only on one side, irreconcilable discrepancies occur mainly between US grants and the corresponding partners' receipts (in 25 cases out of a total of 63 countries, 16 underreporting, 9 overreporting, their receipts from the US); US figures for US grants were entered in the table. In the majority of the discrepancies of the partners' figures with those of the US the discrepancy is 5 per cent or less, or amounts to less than $5 million. In the following cases the discrepancies are over 10 per cent and over $5 million (figures in millions of dollars): Belgium, −63; Netherlands, −69; Israel, −30; Norway, −17; Yugoslavia, +86; India, −11; Indonesia, −7. The Continental OEEC area as a whole underreports its receipts from the US. The amount of $282 million to unallocated OEEC (US column in Group 1) can, therefore, not explain the discrepancies and seems to represent general expenditures of the program.

Loans. Most discrepancies are less than $5 million. In the following cases the discrepancies are over 10 per cent and over $5 million of the net figure (figures in millions of dollars): discrepancies of *liability* figures from US asset figures which were entered in the table — Japan, −20, Mexico, −14; discrepancies of the *asset* figures from the liability figures where the latter figures were taken — repayments by Germany (−30) and France (−58) to Switzerland: the Swiss record falls short by 14 for Germany, and 24 for France, i.e., total discrepancy, +38; Netherlands loan to Belgium (26): Netherlands reports 8, discrepancy, −18; repayment by Indonesia to Netherlands (−8): Netherlands reports +2, discrepancy, +10.

APPENDIX TABLE B-Ia

Types and Purposes of Government Grants and Gross Loans, Five-Year Totals, 1950–54

(*millions of dollars*)

	Group 1	Group 2	Group 3	Group 4	Una	Total
Total	9,041	2,133	3,086	5,536	796	20,592
Grants	7,745	883	1,794	3,365	796	14,583[a]
Loans	1,296	1,250	1,292	2,171		6,009[b]
1. Relief and rehabilitation (WW II)						
Grants	774	6	11	372	201	1,364
a. Civilian supplies: US(729), UK(1) to Ger (185), Jpn(545); RyI(57)	730			57		787
b. Famine relief in WEur and Jpn: US to Ger(17), Ita(19), Aus(5), Jpn(1)	42					42
c. War damage and reconstruction: US to Phil(181); UK to Mal and Bor(61)				242		242
d. Swe grants to Den(3), Nor(3), Ger(2), under Washington Agreement	2	6				8
e. UN, IRO and Can to COEEC for IRO, etc.(11)					119	119
f. UN, UNICEF			10	1	36	47
g. UN, UNRWA			1	72	46	119
Loans						
h. UK to Mal				23		23

(*continued*)

APPENDIX TABLE B-1a (*continued*)

	Group 1	Group 2	Group 3	Group 4	Una	Total
2. Eur and Jpn recovery Grants	6,855	471	26		448	7,800
a. US econ. & techn. assis.: UK(1,673), Aus (390), Bel(261), Fr(1,916), Ger(843), Ita (934), Nth(496), Ice(22), Ire(14), Den (127), Nor(151), Swe(48), Por(13)						
b. Through IEPA-EPU to OEEC countries (except Gr & Tur) and IEPA-EPU net receipts (una)	6,513	362	13		282	7,170
receipts (una)	342	109	13		166	630
Loans	1,181	269	36			1,486
c. General aid: ECA/MSA(381); EXIM (303, including 17 for Den converted from private loan)	537	111	36			684
d. EXIM: cotton(81), tobacco(10) credits	91					91
e. Can loan to UK	45					45
f. Intra-EPU area loans (including EPU and BIS)	185	13				198
g. Intra-Eur consolidations of short-term debts	217	145				362
h. Aid to Jpn: EXIM cotton credit	106					106
3. Grants due to obligations, in the nature of contractual payments	13	166	286	17	3	479
a. Reparations[c]	29	135	279	14	3	454

b. Revaluation of Sterling balances: UK to Uru(13), Bra(23), Por(3), Irn(3)		26	13	3	42
c. Indemnification for loss of oil revenue: Irq to Tur (WW I)			3		3
d. Pal settlement with successor states (UK presumably all to Isr)			18		18
e. Return lend-lease ships: UK(−6), Fr(−10), USSR(−22)			−22	−16	−38
4. Military buildup and military emergencies — Grants	977	4	6	90	1,077
a. Military production and construction: US to UK(44), Fr(30), Ita(8), Nth(2), Nor(4), Tur(6), and Can to UK(6)		4	6	90	100
b. Kor: US civilian relief(440), economic (232), Tha rice(3), UNKRA(98, estimated)	773				773
c. Ich: US only (economic); Fr, n.a.	138				138
d. Mal: UK, internal security measures (Communist guerilla war)	43				43
e. Ken: UK grants for "emergency" and "agricultural resettlement" (Mau-Mau rebellion)	23				23
Loans	72	12	242	29	355
f. US loans for strategic material production (including EXIM loans for this purpose)	67	12	176	29	284
g. UK loan to Can corporation			66		66
h. UK loan to Ken for "emergency"	5				5

(continued)

APPENDIX TABLE B-Ia (*continued*)

	Group 1	Group 2	Group 3	Group 4	Una	Total
5. Aid to strategic countries						
Grants	13		1,349	412		1,774
a. Gr and Tur: US to Gr(550), Tur(186), IEPA-EPU to Gr(179), Tur(57),			972			972
b. Yug: US (economic 302, mil. construction 7), UK(41), Fr(27)			377			377
c. Tai: US (economic 343, student aid 5)				348		348
d. Jor: UK grants only				64		64
e. Ber: US	13					13
Loans			200	12		212
f. Tur: US(70), UK(1), EPU(25)			96			96
g. Yug: US(55), UK(47), Nth(2)			104			104
h. Jor (UK)				12		12
6. Development aid						
Grants		236	39	1,480	131	1,886
a. US economic and technical assistance n.e.c.		223	39	473	22	757
b. UK development aid to RFd(13), Lby (26), dependencies(171)		13		197	35	245
c. Continent to independent countries(13); and to dependencies (Fr 644, Ita 51, Nth 29, Por 1)				738		738
d. Colombo Plan aid by Group 2 (Can 41, Asl 25, NZ 6)				72		72

e. Economic and technical assistance through UN(69) and by US through IIAA(5)					74	74
Loans	86	739	961	2,064		3,850
f. US EXIM and program loans not included elsewhere		291	337	202		830
g. US commodity loans: Ind wheat loan (190); Sp cotton loan(23)			23	190		213
h. Eur loans to independent countries by UK(25) and Nth(53), Swe(1)		13		66		79
i. Eur loans to dependent territories by UK(3); Bel(22); Fr(1,334); Nth(14); Por(16)				1,389		1,389
j. Oth loans: Con to Sabena(2); SAr to Syr(4)	2			4		6
k. US funding of import arrears (Bra 300), Phi short-term debt (35), and conversion from private loans(10)			310	35		345
l. Other consolidations of short-term debts by Arg(5), Bra(9), and refinancing by UK(4)		9		9		18
m. IBRD loans	84	426	291	169		970
7. Natural Disaster Aid						
Grants						
a. US famine relief and agr. commod. programs			77	107		184
b. US: aid to Mex (foot & mouth disease)			31	92		123
			27			27
c. Mis disasters (US to EEur 19; UK to dependencies 14; Gua and others to Ecu 1)			19	15		34

(continued)

APPENDIX TABLE B-Ia (*concluded*)

	Group 1	Group 2	Group 3	Group 4	Una	Total
8. Other						
Grants						
Residual Una					19	19
Loans						
Export loans to SBI by Swe(80); NZ(3)			83			83
9. Recapitulation:						
US grants and loans						
All categories excluding development aid (lines 1 through 5 and 7)						
Grants	7,365	366	1,119	1,488	282	10,620
Loans	763	287	173	67		1,290
Total	8,128	653	1,292	1,555	282	11,910
Development aid (line 6)						
Grants		223	39	473	27	762
Loans		291	670	427		1,388
Total		514	709	900	27	2,150
All other countries						
All categories excluding development aid (lines 1 through 5, 7, and 8)						
Grants	380	281	625	226	193	1,705
Loans	447	224	158	40		869
Total	827	505	783	266	193	2,574

Development aid (line 6)						
Grants		13		1,007	35	1,055
Loans	2	22		1,468		1,492
Total	2	35		2,475	35	2,547
IntI						
UN relief grants (line 1)			11	171	190	372
UN development grants (line 6)					69	69
Total			11	171	259	441
IBRD development loans (line 6)	84	426	291	169		970

NOTES TO APPENDIX TABLE B-Ia

[a] The grand total differs from that in Appendix Table B-I by redonated receipts of UN and IEPA-EPU ($1,146 million).

[b] Gross loans have been entered here, while in Appendix Table B-I loans are shown net. Repayments amounted to: government loans $3,637 million; IBRD Loans $106 million.

[c] See Appendix Table B-I.

n.a. = not available.

n.e.c. = not elsewhere classified.

NOTE: See the List of Abbreviations at the end of Appendix B.

APPENDIX TABLE B-II

Portfolio Investment, New Issues, Redemptions and Trading, Five-Year Totals, 1950–54

(*millions of dollars*)

Borrowers		Total	Group 1 Total	US	UK	COEEC & Jpn	Other Groups
Total	Total portfolio	2,401	2,475	848	797	830	−74
	Issues	3,125	2,991	1,610	713	668	134
	R & T	−724	−516	−762	84	162	−208
Group 1	Total portfolio	232	423	19	223	181	−191
	Issues	70	70			70	
	R & T	162	353	19	223	111	−191
US	Issues	17	17			Swi 17	
	R & T	364	377		246	Nth −124, Swi[a] 225, Jpn 1, Uni 29	Can −94, Oth[b] 81
UK	R & T	−183	−8	−8			
Aus	R & T	−15	−15	−9	−6		Ire −131
Bel	Issues	32	32			Swi 32	
	R & T	−16	−16	−14	−2		Oth[c] −44

(*continued*)

APPENDIX TABLE B-II (continued)

| | | Lenders | | | | Other Groups |
| | | Group 1 | | | | |
Borrowers	Total	Total	US	UK	COEEC & Jpn	
Group 1 (cont.)						
Fr						
Issues	9	9			Swi 9	
R & T	-15	-19		-7	Nth -12 [d]	Leb 3 [d]; Egy 1
Ger						
R & T	-16	-16			Fr -3 [d]; Uni -13	
Ita						
R & T	-21	-21	-9	-12		
Nth						
Issues	12	12			Swi 12	
R & T	172	152	102	9 [d]	Fr -8 [d]; Uni 49	Ins -9; Una 29
Swi						
R & T	-56	-56	-31		Fr -25 [d]; Nth -8	Mis [e] -27
UniOEEC						
R & T	-35	-8				
Jpn						
R & T	-17	-17	-12	-5		
Group 2						
Total portfolio	1,175	1,156	644	351	161	19
Issues	1,673	1,653	1,179	385	89	20
R & T	-498	-497	-535	-34	72	-1
Can						
Issues	993	993	993			
R & T	-336	-332	-384	-35	Fr -5 [d]; Uni 92	
Chi						
R & T	-23	-23	-12	-9	Uni -2	SAf 2; Una -6

		1	2	3		
Isr	Issues	172	172	172		Una −6
	R & T	−17	−11	−11		
Ire	Issues	4	4			
	R & T	40	40	40		
Asl	Issues	27	27	14	Swi 13	NZ 16
	R & T	−96	−112	−68	Uni 4	
NZ	Issues	44	44	44		Asl −4; SAf 1; UniRSA −11[f]
	R & T	−22	−8	−8		
RFd	Issues	203	203	203		
	R & T	−6	−10	−10		
SAf	Issues	171	171	120	Swi 51	SAf 4
	R & T	135	113	75	Bel 13; Fr 8; Nth 1	Can 2; RFd 9; UKOT 4; UniRSA 7
Den	R & T	−67	−64	−5	Uni −8	Can −1; Una −2
Nor	Issues	34	14	14		Swe 20
	R & T	−71	−55	−7	Uni −29	Swe −16
Swe	Issues	25	25		Swi 25	
	R & T	−14	−12	−11	Uni −2	
Fin	R & T	−14	−5	−4		Fin −1; UniRSA −1
Arg	R & T	−1	−12	−12		Swe −2; Una −7[d]
Uru	R & T	−6	−6			Una 11

(continued)

APPENDIX TABLE B-II (*concluded*)

Borrowers		Total	Total	US	UK	COEEC & Jpn	Other Groups
					Group 1		
					Lenders		
Group 3	Total portfolio	-192	-203	-82	-120	-1	11
	Issues	10	10	10			
	R & T	-202	-213	-92	-120	-1	11
Bra	R & T	-138	-140	-34	-110	Uni 4	UniLA 2
Col	R & T	-10	-10	-10			
Cub	R & T	-8	-8	-8			
Mex	R & T	-8	-17	-17			Can 9
Pan	Issues	10	10	10			
	R & T	-9	-9	-9			
Ven	R & T	-	-	-2		Swi 2	
Gr	R & T	-1	-1	-1			
Por	R & T	4	4	4			
Tur	R & T	-15	-15		-10	Fr -5	
Sp	R & T	-17	-17	-15		Fr -2 [d]	
Group 4	Total portfolio	608	611	-47	313	345	
	Issues	647	647		295	352	
	R & T	-39	-36	-47	18	-7	
CR	R & T	-1	-1	-1			-3
Dom	R & T	1	1	1			-3

Place	Type	I	II	III	IV	Creditor breakdown
EIS	R & T	-3	-3	-1	-2	
Hon	R & T	-1	-1	-1	-1	
Nic	R & T	-1	-1			
Per	Issues	2	2			Swi 2
Phi	R & T[g]	-14	-14	-14		
Cey	Issues	14	14		14	
Ind	R & T[h]	33	38	1	32	Ger 4; Swi 1; Can -1; Pak -9; Una 5
UKOT	Issues[i]	281	281	-21	281	SAf 2; -6
Ins	R & T[i]	-25	-27	-5	-6	
Tha	R & T	-5	-5	-3		
Egy	R & T	-3	-3	1		Fr -3
Par	R & T	-7	-7	-2	-5	
COT	Issues	-2	-2	-2		350; -9
BelC	R & T	350	350			Bel 82; Swi 41
BelC	Issues	-11	-11	-2		Bel -9
FrOT	R & T	123	123			Fr 227
IBRD	Issues	-11	-11		33	Nth 11; Swi 136; Jpn[k] 10; Can 43; Mis[k] 71
IBRD	Issues[j]	725	611	421		227
Una & tax havens	R & T	-100	-103	-92	-3	Swi -8; Can 3
Una & tax havens	R & T	-47	-20	-15		Nth -5; SAf 1; IBRD -28

NOTES TO APPENDIX TABLE B-II

a Includes (1) transactions in US Government securities which, judging by US data, appear to be small; (2) liabilities of an unknown nature.

b Chile 4, Israel −4, Ireland 1, Australia −1, New Zealand −1, South Africa 2, Sweden −6, Argentina −3; Brazil 4, Colombia −2, Cuba 13, Mexico 6, Venezuela 11, Spain −1; Guatemala −2, Bolivia 1, Peru 1, Philippines −2, Taiwan −2, Hong Kong 13, Indonesia −1, Continental OT 2; Unalloc.: RSA 2, Latin America 14; tax havens: Panama 11, Western Europe and Africa 23.

c Canada −10, Australia −7, New Zealand −42 (may include transactions other than portfolio, but not direct investment), South Africa 14, Rhodesian Federation 4, Norway 1, Sweden −2; Sudan −2.

d These entries were assumed to consist of portfolio transactions, although they may include other types of capital.

e Canada 2, Australia −1, South Africa 2, Norway 9; repurchases of IBRD obligations −39.

f May include transactions other than portfolio, but not direct investment.

g The Philippine redemption was connected with a funding operation and is not a net repayment.

h Not true portfolio, as explained in the text.

i Issues: Cyprus 11; Br. E. Africa 180; Br. W. Africa 28; Aden 3; Mauritius 7; Malaya 11; Br. Guiana 6; Br. W. Indies 35. Redemptions & Trading: by US from Hong Kong −21; by UK from other OT −6.

j The distribution of IBRD issues corresponds to the amounts taken by the lenders and differs from the amounts floated in the respective markets. Flotations by market were as follows: US 585, UK 28, Netherlands 11, Switzerland 66, Canada 35.

k Purchases of IBRD bonds by central banks: S. Africa 7, Cuba 18, Mexico 4, El Salvador 4, Honduras 5, Nicaragua 3, Ethiopia 22, Thailand 8; the Japanese purchase was also a central bank purchase; the amounts of Japan, Thailand, and Mexico are estimates.

R & T is redemptions and trading.

NOTE: See the List of Abbreviations at the end of Appendix B.

Portfolio issues — Flotations in US represent the amounts taken in US (for IBRD issues by market, see note *j*); exclude small issues, mainly of Canadian origin but the amounts involved are said to be small. Flotations in London exclude refunding issues; these amounted to $120 million, but are not identifiable by country or area. There are no discrepancies.

Portfolio redemptions and trading — Discrepancies (after adjustments, if any) over 10 per cent and over $5 million: (1) Discrepancies of the *liability* figures from the asset figures in cases where the latter figures were entered in the table, US (for which transactions in US securities were based on partner data) with Canada −29, with Latin America +14, France with Switzerland +25 (not reported by France); Canada with US +296 (offset by a discrepancy in Appendix Table B-III, see notes to that table); Denmark with US +9; Mexico with Canada −9 (not reported by Mexico). (2) Discrepancies of the *asset* figures from the liability figures in cases where the latter figures were entered in the table: UK with Canada −55; France with Turkey +7; New Zealand with Australia −17 (possibly due to time lag); Pakistan with India −9 (not reported by Pakistan).

APPENDIX TABLE B-III

Direct Investment, Five-Year Totals, 1950–54

(millions of dollars)

		Lenders						
			Group 1				Groups 2, 3, 4 and Unallocated	
Borrowers	Total	Total	US	UK	COEEC & Jpn	Total Other	Can	Other
Total	11,492	10,601	6,865	2,459	1,277	891	623	268
Group 1	2,792	2,189 ᵃ	1,128	428	633 ᵃ	603 ᵃ	548	55 ᵃ
US	1,402	864		391	Fr 30 ᵇ / Nth 257 / Swi 119 / Uni 64 / Jpn 3	538	512	Isr 3 / NZ 4 / SAf 1 / Den 1 / Bra −7 / OthEur 1 / UKOT 1 / Una 22
UK	621	573	527		Nth 46 ᵇ	48	30	Asl 8 / NZ 1 / SAf 7 / Den 2
Aus	15	15	15					
Bel	69	69	69					

(continued)

APPENDIX TABLE B-III *(continued)*

Borrowers	Total	Lenders						
		Group 1				Groups 2, 3, 4 and Unallocated		
		Total	US	UK	COEEC & Jpn	Total Other	Can	Other
Group 1 (cont.)								
Fr	197	190	144	27[b]	Bel 1[b] Swi 18[b]	7	4	Swe 2[b] Por 1[b]
Ger	135	135	94		Uni 41			
Ita	128	124	84	3	Fr 7 Uni 30	4		UniLA 4
Nth	101	101	81		Uni 20			
Swi	14	14	14					
Jpn	110	108	100	7	Nth 1	2	2	
Group 2	5,126	4,973	3,616	1,088	269	153	14	139
Can	3,172	3,170	2,897	186	Uni 87	2		Una 2
Chi	124	124	124					
Isr	92	92	49		Uni 43			
Asl	737	721	228	459	Uni 34	16	5	NZ 10 SAf 1
NZ	117	104	18	81	Uni 5	13		Asl 13
RFd	109	59	15	44[c]		50		SAf 50

Country					Destination breakdown
SAf	416	389	111	262	Bel 1, Fr 3, Ger 6, Nth 4, Swi 2; 27; 6; Asl 3, NZ 2, RFd 7, Den 1, UniRSA 6, COT 2
Den	22	22	10	2	Uni 10
Nor	132	131	18	54	Uni 59; 1; 3; UniLA −2
Swe	33	33	33		
Fin	22	24	10		Uni 14; −2; Una −2
Arg	83	83	83		
Uru	67	21	20		Fr 1; 46; Una 46
Group 3					
Bra	1,444	1,357	1,238	40	Fr 79; 87; 59; Una 28
Col	465	463	450		Uni 13; 2; 1; Una 1, Ven −7, Ecu 4
	66	69	69		−3
Cub	132	132	132 [d]	27	
Mex	306	223	156		Fr 2, Ger 20, Uni 18; 83; 56; Swe 27
Pan	52	52	52	13	
Ven	352	347	326		Fr 7, Ity 1; 5; 2; Arg 1, Pan 2
Gr	5	5	5		Uni 10
Tur	28	28	18		Fr 1 [b]
Por	14	14	9		Uni 4 [e]
Sp	21	21	21		
Leb	3	3			Fr 3

(continued)

APPENDIX TABLE B-III (*concluded*)

Borrowers	Total	Lenders						
		Group 1				Groups 2, 3, 4 and Unallocated		
		Total	US	UK	COEEC & Jpn	Total Other	Can	Other
Group 4	2,130	2,082	883	903	296	48	2	46
CR	2	2	2					
Dom	30	30	30					
ElS	2	2	2					
Gua	2	2	2					
Hai	13	13	4		Fr 9			
Hon	41	41	41					
Nic	4	4	4					
Ecu	13	10	7	3		3		Una 3
Per	91	90	85	−2	Uni 7	1		UniLA 1
UnaCA	11	11	11[f]					
Phi	102	85	85			17		Una 17
Tai	14	14	14					
SAr	260	260	260					
Lib	34	34	34					
Ind	295	304	65	235	Ger 1 Swi 2 Jpn 1	−9	3	NZ −1 Bur −3 Cey −1 Una −7

Pak	26	26	3	22[g]	Uni 1	6	UniME 6
Irq	50	44	10	21	Fr 10 · Uni 3		
Ins	−5	−5	−7				
Eth	19	19	4		Nth 2		
Sud	6	6	5	1	Nth & Fr 15		
UKOT	766	766	155	611			
WHem	190	190	48	142[h]			
Af & Ade	367	367	34	333			
ME, FE, & Oth	111	111	73	38			
Una	98	98		98[i]			h
AslOT	31					31	Asl 31
Par	9	9	9			2	
Egy	37	35	14	13	Fr 2 · Uni 6 · Fr 1	2	UniME 2
Syr	1	1				−3	UniSA −2
COT	276	279	44	−1	236 · Bel 28 · Uni −4	3	3
BelC	31	28	4				
NthOT	16	42	19	−1	Nth 24 · Fr 185 · Nth 2 · Swi 1	−26	Una −26 · SAf 2
FrOT	222	205	17			17	UniSA 16
PorOT	7	4	4			3	Una 3

NOTES TO APPENDIX TABLE B-III

[a] The total of the Group 1 receipts from the Continent is smaller by 4, and the total Group 1 receipts from other is larger by 4, then the sums of the entries in the columns. This amount represents Danish investment in unidentified OEEC presumably included in the unidentified receipts of the Continental countries.

[b] For these entries there is some doubt as to the type of capital. They were included here because, all considered, they are most likely to consist, entirely or largely, of direct investment but they may include other private capital.

[c] Mainly investment in mining in 1950 and 1951. After that year the mining companies moved their head offices from London to Salisbury, and their subsequent investment appears as portfolio.

[d] Includes 42 United States Government investments.

[e] United Kingdom and Cont. OEEC, liabilities net of assets.

[f] United States Government investment in abaca plantations.

[g] Underestimated by changes in intercompany accounts and imports of equipment; may include portfolio.

[h] A discrepancy of +31 of Canadian investment in Sterling Area may represent investment in Jamaica, in which case the United Kingdom investment in Western Hemisphere UKOT would be smaller by 31.

[i] Investment by United Kingdom Overseas Food and Colonial Development Corporations.

NOTE: See the List of Abbreviations at the end of Appendix B.

Discrepancies (after adjustments, if any) of partners' figures from those entered in the table, where the partner's figure diverges from the entered figure both by more than 10 per cent and by more than $5 million, are as follows: (1) Discrepancies of the *liability* figures from the asset figures in cases where the latter figures were entered in the table (these discrepancies are all with the United States asset figures which were used for all entries in the United States column), France +35; Japan −13; Canada −386; Brazil −120; Colombia +22; Mexico +114; Haiti +11; Ecuador +6; Peru +44; Philippines +36; India −8; Paraguay −7; Continental OT −6. (2) Discrepancies of the *asset* figures from the liability figures in cases where the latter figures were entered in the table (the country or countries whose figures were entered and with which the discrepancy occurs appear in parentheses): Belgium +10 (with Congo); Canada −189 (with US), +6 (with Continent), +31 (with rest of Sterling Area—but see note *h*), −26 (with Latin America).

The large discrepancies of Canada with the United States seem to originate mainly in different definitions of types of capital. The United States counts purchases of securities of a direct investment enterprise by all residents of the investor's country as direct, while Canada counts only those of the controlling interests, the remainder as portfolio. The discrepancy of −386 is, consequently, largely offset by a positive discrepancy in portfolio. There are other differences in treatment as well, resulting in offsetting discrepancies in the various types. The over-all net discrepancy of all United States-Canadian movements is far smaller. Since for most entries the United States figures were used, there is little possibility of duplication or omission of movements between the two countries.

The Mexican discrepancy seems largely due to the inclusion in the Mexican record of investment by resident foreigners (see United States Department of Commerce, *Investment in Mexico,* Washington, D.C., 1955, p. 11). The reasons for the other large discrepancies could not be ascertained.

Inclusion of reinvested profits: Reinvested profits are included for—all transactions of the United States; the transactions of the following Sterling Area countries: Australia, New Zealand, India, Iraq, United Kingdom OT for 1953 and 1954; and for the British investment in Rhodesia; the transactions of the following Latin American countries: Mexico, Venezuela, Peru, Haiti, Ecuador, and possibly some others; the transactions of Japan; the Philippines; and among the OEEC countries apparently only Denmark.

Possible effect on the distribution of omitted reinvested profits: Reinvested profits are excluded in a number of cases where they may have been important. In Group 1 there was probably more British investment in petroleum marketing facilities, since the British companies had shares in all the Continental markets. Intra-Continental investment may also have been somewhat larger. In Group 2 the missing reinvested profits of the United Kingdom and Continent in Canada and South Africa may have been substantial. For South Africa, the 1956 Census figures put cumulative reinvested profits at 38 per cent of total value. British investment in South Africa alone may have been larger by $150 million or more. There may have been some reinvestment in Latin America, particularly in Argentina (Group 2) and Brazil (Group 3), where British investment was still of some size. In Group 4, the countries where excluded reinvested profits may have been of some size are Pakistan, Indonesia, and the Continental dependencies, particularly the French.

All groups are thus affected by the omission of reinvested profits in certain cases. Considering the possible magnitudes involved, it is unlikely that the distribution among recipient groups would be substantially altered. The shares in the total supply of the United Kingdom and the Continent would be somewhat increased, perhaps by 2 per cent for the United Kingdom, and by somewhat less for the Continent.

APPENDIX TABLE B-IV

Loans by the Private Sector, and Repayments, Five-Year Totals, 1950–54

(*millions of dollars*)

Borrowers	Total Loans	Total Repayments	Lenders — Total Loans	Lenders — Total Repayments	Group 1 US Loans	Group 1 US Repayments	Group 1 UK Loans	Group 1 UK Repayments	Group 1 Switzerland Loans	Group 1 Switzerland Repayments	Group 1 OthCOEEC Loans	Group 1 OthCOEEC Repayments	Other & Unallocated Loans	Other & Unallocated Repayments
Total	1,649	1,427	1,531	1,267	1,042	664	73	133	173	80	243	390	118	160
Net	222		264		378		−60		93		−147		−42	
Group 1	787	784	765	741	542	281	5	68	149	68	69	324	22	43
Net	3		24		261		−63		81		−255		−21	
US	23	12	13	3			5	3	8				Can 1, Den 3, Nor 3, Sp 3, UniLA 3	1, 4, 1, 3
UK	191	48	179	27	179	11					Fr	16[a]	SAf 4, Den 1, Nor 8	1, 20
Aus	9	8	9	8					8	2	Ger 1	4		
Bel	73	168	73	168	43	53			30	15	Fr[b]	115[a]		
Fr	260	165	260	152	200	133			60		Ger	4[a]	Leb, Syr	6, 7
Ger	75	148	75	148	1	36		65	18[c]	7	Fr, Nth 56[c], Uni	22, 18[a]		

	1	2	3	4	5	6	7	8	9	10	11	12	13	14
Ita	28	37	28	37	5	5	23	32			Fr[b] 50		86	109
Nth	23	85	23	85	22	23	1	12			Fr[b] 21			−23
Swi	1	23	1	23	1	2					Fr[b] 74			
UniCOEEC	12	74	12	74	1						Nth 12[c]			
Jpn	92	16	92	16	91	16	24		56			50		
Group 2	396	337	310	228	180	129				60		31		
Net	59		82		51		16	8	−4		19		−23	
Can	62	50	39	46	30	15			18	2	Uni 7	13	Una 23	4
Chi	66	46	66	46	58	44			2	2	Uni[d] 6			
Isr	83	27	69	23	41	17	9		6	2	Aus 7	4	Can 4	
											Bel 6		Swe 10	4
Ice	2	1	2	1	1	1					Uni 1			
Asl	1		1		1									
RFd	2													
SAf	91	24	91	23	30	12	15	8	46	3			SAf 2	1
Den	11	17	11	17	10	17					Nth 11[c]		Den	
Nor	10	68	10	45	6	10			35					
Swe	52	76	6	7		2					Fr 5[a]		Swe	23
											Bel 7	7	Nor 46[e]	69[e]
Fin	13	23	12	15		6					Fr 2	2	Nor 1	
											Nth 3		Swe	8
Arg	3	1	3	1	3	1				1				
Uru	4	4	4	4	251	4			12	4			10	7
Group 3	382	255	372	248	206	206		−4	7	5	109	33		3
Net	127		124		45	45					76			
Bra	123	56	123	54	82	38			1		Uni[d] 40	16	Una	2
Col	97	52	90	51	43	45			1		Bel 2		Swe	5
											Fr 30		UniLA 2	1
Cub	38	10	38	10	38	10					Uni[d] 14	16		
Mex	65	50	65	50	55	50					Uni[d] 10			
Pan	5	14	5	14	5	14								
Ven	14	10	14	10	4	5		5	10	5		16		

(continued)

APPENDIX TABLE B-IV (concluded)

Lenders

	Total		Group 1											
			Total		US		UK		Switzerland		OthCOEEC		Other & Unallocated	
Borrowers	Loans	Repay-ments	Loans	Repay-ments	Loans	Repay-ments	Loans	Repay-ments	Loans	Repay-ments	Loans	Repay-ments	Loans	Repay-ments
Group 3 (cont.)														
Gr	6		6		2						Uni 4			
Tur	2	5	1	5							Aus 1 / Fr	1 / 4	Isr 1	1
Sp	22	40	22	40	22	40					Aus 8	1		
Yug	8	9	8	9		4				4				
SB1	2	9		5							Fr 15	5 / 2	Nor 2	4 / 1
Group 4	84	51	84	50	69	48								
Net	33		34		21							13		−1
CR	2	1	2	1	2	1								
Hai	3	1	3	1	3	1								
Hon		1		1		1								
Nic	10	5	10	5	2	3					Ger 8	2		
Bol	31	25	31	25	31	25								
Ecu	7	1	7		1									
Per	10	6	10	6	10	6					Fr 6		Col & Ven	1
Tai	8	5	8	5	8	5								
Lib	10	7	10	7	10	7								
Ins	1		1											
UKOT	1		1		1									
BelC	1		1		1						Fr 1			

NOTES TO APPENDIX TABLE B-IV

[a] These transactions are not unambiguously identified by type of capital. They were included here because, considering all the available evidence, they are most likely to consist, entirely or largely, of private loan transactions.

[b] France (whose regional distribution distinguishes only currencies) reported receipts of repayments of 210 million in dollars. There are no corresponding entries in the accounts of Dollar Area countries. On the other hand, several Continental countries report repayments which, by timing, coincide with the French entries, *viz.*, the Netherlands (50), Switzerland (21), both made to "Continental OEEC," which we assumed to correspond to the French figure; in addition, we attributed half (65) of Belgium's unallocated residual of its net private capital outflow to Appendix Table B-IV and counted it against the French entry (included in the amount of 115, 50 of which is identified as a repayment to France in the French record). This procedure leaves 74 of the French receipts unaccounted for, which we entered as a repayment by "Unidentified Continental OEEC" on the assumptions that it came mainly from these countries. (See also footnote *a*.)

[c] Loans to Unidentified Continental OEEC countries are reported by the Netherlands (79) and Switzerland (5); loans received from unidentified Continental OEEC countries are reported by Germany (61) and Denmark (11). The Swiss loans (5 included in 18) and part of the Netherlands loans (56) were assumed to correspond to the German entry, and 11 of the Netherlands loans were assumed to be the loans to Denmark, leaving a residual of 12 of the Netherlands loans to "Unidentified Continental OEEC."

[d] The loans received by Latin American countries from "Unidentified Continental OEEC" (total 70, repayments −22) are partly accounted for (18 and −6) by loans reported by the Netherlands to have been made to (unidentified) Latin America.

[e] The loans (46) and repayments (−69) reported by Norway for prepayments of ships (and repayment through delivery of ships) were assumed to have been to Sweden (which did not record private loan transactions) because much of the reconstruction of the Norwegian fleet took place in Swedish yards.

NOTE: See the List of Abbreviations at the end of Appendix B.

Discrepancies (after adjustments, if any) of partners' figures from those entered in the table: (1) Discrepancies of the *liability* figures from the asset figures in cases where the latter were entered in the table—Canada reports loans of 26 from, and repayments of −39 to, the United States, net discrepancy −28, but the Canadian figure may include other transactions. Other discrepancies were negligible. (2) Discrepancies of the *asset* figures ·from the liability figures in cases where the latter figures were entered in the table—United States loans were broken down largely from partner data. United States discrepancy with partner data for repayments, +74, attributable to German repayment (36) under the London debt agreement, which is not in the United States record; and to Latin America (27) and Other. These may be due to time lags since some large repayments were made in 1954. Switzerland reported total repayments of only 69, discrepancy, +11. Other discrepancies were negligible.

APPENDIX TABLE B-V

Extraordinary Repatriations, Five-Year Totals, 1950-54

(millions of dollars)

Borrowers	Total	Lenders				
		Group 1				Groups 2, 3, 4
		Total	US	UK	COEEC	
Total	−627	−563	−56	−399	−108	−64
Group 1	−84	−51		−11	−40	−33
US (n.s.)	−2					Egy −2
UK (n.s.)	−28					Ind −19, Egy −9
Fr (n.s.)	−24				Ita −24[a]	
Ger (real estate)	−27			−11	Uni −16	
UniOEEC (n.s.)	−3					Yug −1, Egy −2
Group 2	−13			−13		
Uru (water supply)	−13			−13		

Group 3						
Bra (railroad)	−165	−163		−77	−31	−2
Cub (railroad)	−32	−32		−32		
Mex (petroleum, agriculture)	−12	−12	−55	−12		
	−68	−68	−55	−13		
Ven (telephone)	−10	−10		−10		
Gr (agriculture)	−2	−2		−2		
Leb (urban transit)	−5	−5			Fr −5; Bel −1; Fr −5; Ita −16[a]; Swi −4	Swe −2
Yug (n.s.)	−36	−34		−8		
Group 4						
Bol (mining)	−365	−336		−298	−37	−29
Dom (n.s.)	−3	−3		−3		
Phi (railroad)	−1	−1		−13		Ind −10
Bur (petroleum; n.s.)	−13	−13		−8		Ind −4
	−18	−8				
Cey (agriculture; n.s.)	−31	−27		−27		
Ind[b]	−209	−209		−209		
Ins (n.s.)	−20	−20			Nth −20	
Eth (n.s.)	−3	−3			Ita −3[a]	
Sud (agriculture)	−15	−15		−15	Fr −4	UniME −4
Egy (n.s.)	−39	−35		−21	Umi −10	
Par (power, banking)	−6					Bra −4
UniME (n.s.)	−7	−2		−2		Egy −7

a Liquidation of Italian investment in settlement of reparations (therefore offset in Appendix Table B-I).

b Miscellaneous: commercial enterprises including tea estates ($55 million); transfers of savings of departing British personnel ($154 million); both amounts may include other remittances.

n.s. = not specified.

NOTE: See the List of Abbreviations at the end of Appendix B.

Discrepancies (after adjustments, if any) of partners' figures from those entered in the table: (1) Discrepancies of the *asset* figures from the liability figures in cases where the latter figures were entered in the table—United States repatriations from Mexico, United States acknowledges only −42, discrepancy, +13. Repatriations from Yugoslavia, acknowledged by Italy, −20, discrepancy, −4; Switzerland, −15, discrepancy, −11; Sweden, 0, discrepancy, +2. Repatriations to India, the Indian record shows an inflow of $89 million from Asian countries, according to exchange control data. This amount is assumed in the balance of payments to be repatriation of Indian capital. It is said to originate in Malaya and "other nearby countries" (Reserve Bank of India, *Survey of India's Foreign Liabilities and Assets as on 31st December 1953*, Bombay, 1955, p. 83). Burma and Ceylon acknowledge 14 of this amount. The residual of 75, presumably mainly from Malaya, we excluded on the grounds that it probably consisted mainly of private remittance by Indian laborers, rather than capital repatriation. "Rough estimates" for such remittance are also included in the balance of payments, but not based on the exchange control record, and these may, therefore, be incomplete or duplicated (see IMF, *Balance of Payments Yearbook*, Vol. 8, Indian account, notes to items 9 and 13). (2) Discrepancies of the *liability* figures from the asset figures in cases where the latter figures were entered in the tables—The liquidation of Italian investment in settlement of reparations in Continental OEEC was assumed to be France (24), since the other possible partner, Greece, acknowledges only reparations in kind and in cash. The French record (based on exchange control data) does not include this amount.

APPENDIX TABLE B-VI

Net Short-Term Credit, Country Data

(*millions of dollars*)

	Total Net Outflow or Inflow (1)	Funding of Debt (off-set entries) (2)	EPU Credit or Debit Balances (3)	IMF Purchases or Repurchases (4)	Special Movements (5)	Residual Credit (6)
Group 1	−319	140	−334	−350	473	−248
United States	77	35		1	453	−412
United Kingdom	192	69	336	−298	−25	110
Continent	−600	36	−670	−116	45	105
Austria	−54		−53			−1
Belgium	(95)	138	−142	−21		120
France	(−90)		243	−20		−313
Germany	(−602)	−102	−489			−11
Italy	480		109			371
Netherlands	−454		−168	−75	45	−256
Switzerland	(25)		−170			195
Japan	12			63		−51

(*continued*)

APPENDIX TABLE B-VI (*concluded*)

	Total Net Outflow or Inflow (1)	Funding of Debt (off-set entries) (2)	EPU Credit or Debit Balances (3)	IMF Pur-chases or Repurchases (4)	Special Move-ments (5)	Residual Credit (6)
Group 2	−41	−114	154	−19	−330	268
US-oriented	−361			4	−355	−10
UK-oriented	45		6	−16	25	30
Denmark	95	−75	101			69
Norway	84	−63	94	−10		63
Sweden	−25	24	−47			−2
Finland	19			3		16
Argentina	47					47
Uruguay	55					55
Group 3	990	2	21	72	90	805
Brazil	273			28		245
Colombia	138			25		113
Other US-or. LA	3					3
Greece	138				90	48
Portugal	64	2	−10			72
Turkey	305		31	19		255
Yugoslavia	86					86
Other Cont.-or.	−17					−17

Group 4	117					214
US-oriented LA	−44	−35		−22	−40	−47
Philippines	−70	−35		3		−35
Taiwan & Korea	71				5	66
India	−65			−47		−18
Indonesia	64			15	−45	94
Other UK-or.	28			9		19
Paraguay	8			1		7
Egypt	45					48
Syria	36			−3		36
COT	44					44
EPU	159		159			–
BIS	−46					−46
IMF	321			321		–
Fleets & tax havens	17		–			17
Discrep.	1,198	−7		2	193	1,010

SOURCE: Country accounts.

NOTE: If there is a net inflow, there is no sign before the figure; if a net outflow, a minus sign.

Because the purpose of this table is to show the distribution of short-term credit and the cases where the larger cumulative inflows occurred, the countries with larger transactions are shown separately, those with moderate movements have been combined. The flows are shown net (changes in assets minus changes in liabilities) for reasons explained in the text.

The explanations of the figures in the columns and of the discrepancies follow.

Column 1: Total reported (and, where possible, adjusted) inflows and outflows. Elimination from these data of reserve movements in Continental currencies totalling −$23 million, reported by the UK and other countries, was spread over four possible partner countries (figures in parentheses).

Columns 2 to 5 show various special transactions, which are explained below, included in column 1; column 6 shows the residual, after the elimination of these transactions, representing largely trade credit.

Column 2: Contra-entries to long-term loans included in Table B-I which represent fundings of short-term balances. The amounts converted to long-term loans appear therefore as short-term repayments by the debtors and as receipts by the creditors. These debt consolidations took place between EPU members at the inception of EPU, but also included is the funding of a US short-term credit to the Philippines.

Column 3: Cumulative credit (−) and debit (+) balances of members with EPU, through which the major part of intra-OEEC trade was cleared, partly by payments in dollars and gold, partly by the extension of these balances. Credit balances exceeded debit balances, resulting in a net receipt by EPU.

Column 4: Currency transactions, purchases (+) or repurchases (−), with the IMF, which resulted in net repayments (repurchases) to the Fund.

Column 5: Transactions other than credit. The net inflow into the US mainly from Canada (Gr. 2, US-oriented) seems to have consisted chiefly of liquid funds. The other transactions cover the following: repatriations of various funds from Indonesia to the Netherlands, from unidentified countries to Greece, from the UK to Ireland (Gr. 2, UK-oriented); dividends declared but not paid by Rhodesia (Gr. 2, UK-oriented), owed to the UK; and currency payments for smuggled imports by Taiwan.

Discrepancy: Since the algebraic sum of the net flows of all countries should be equal to zero, the positive sum of column 1 is the discrepancy between the data (identical with the discrepancy shown in Table 2), which indicates nonreported outflows of that magnitude. As explained in the text, this discrepancy was assumed to consist largely of the nonreported credits extended by the Continental OEEC countries of Group 1 (except for the discrepancies of columns 2–5; the discrepancy of column 5 consists of the US-Canadian discrepancy and the missing partner data of Greece and Taiwan). In other words, it was assumed that the Continent had a much larger outflow than that shown in column 1, and a large outflow instead of the inflow appearing in column 6. In Table 1 the figure for the Continent was therefore built up from the receipts of the other groups and the net figures here were ignored. For this reason the Group 1 figure in this table cannot be reconciled with that in Table 1, but the net figures for Groups 2, 3, and 4 are consistent with the respective gross figures in Table 1. See also the notes to Table 1.

APPENDIX TABLE B-VII

Changes in Reserves and Correspondent Accounts, Five-Year Totals, 1950–54

(*millions of dollars*)

Lenders (holders of currencies)	Total Currency Holdings	Borrowers (currencies held)				Total Gold and Currencies
		US Dollar Reserves	UK Sterling Reserves	Other[a] Currencies	Gold	
Total	6,942	4,964	1,251	727	1,930	8,872
Group 1	3,754	3,397	-8	365	141	3,895
US	159		135	24	-2,770	-2,611
UK	-156	-86		-70	1,200	1,044
Cont	2,917	2,843	-331	405	1,710	4,627
Aus	283	287	b	-4	7	290
Bel	16	-87	b	103	78	94
Fr	542	694	-94	58	53	595
Ger	1,218	1,218			626	1,844
Ita	35	216	-194	13	91	126
Nth	-57	28	-43	-42	565	508
Swi	166	166	n.a.	n.a.	9	(175)
Uni deposits w/BIS	357			357		357
BIS	214	214			128	342
ECCS	36			36		36
EPU	107	107			153	260
Jpn	834	640	188	6	1	835

(*continued*)

APPENDIX TABLE B-VII (*continued*)

Lenders (holders of currencies)	Borrowers (currencies held)					Total Gold and Currencies
	Total Currency Holdings	US Dollar Reserves	UK Sterling Reserves	Other[a] Currencies	Gold	
Group 2	703	516	121	66	1,169	1,872
Can	331	298	32	1	584	915
Chi	−1	−1			3	2
Isr	−59	43	−102			−59
Ice	2	4	−2			2
Ire	−29	−3	−26			−29
Asl	76	−5	83	−2	50	126
NZ	90	−4	99	−5	6	96
RFd	97		97		2	99
SAf	36	25	−2	13	72	108
Den	80	65	7	8		80
Nor	47	34	−1	14	−7	40
Swe	−6	59	−63	−2	195	189
Fin	100	17	44	39	25	125
Arg	−76	−41	−35		155	79
Uru	15	25	−10		84	99
Group 3	176	323	−189	42	241	417
Bra	−302	−110	−192		5	−297
Col	131	131			34	165
Cub	82	64[c]		18	−113	−31
Mex	93	89[c]		4	10	103
Pan	1	1[c]				1

Ven	8	8	−1	2	31	39
Gr	76	75	b	−5	5	81
Por	29	34	b	23	251	280
Tur	22	−1		3	−11	11
Sp	59	56	4		−29	30
Yug	9	5		−3	8	17
Leb	−3				50	47
SBl	−29	−29	d		n.a.	(−29)
Group 4 Independent	−61	379	−434	−6	28	−33
CR	8	8			8	8
Dom	25	25		4	11	33
ElS	−3	−7				8
Gua	1	1			−1	1
Hai	13	13^c		5		12
Hon	8	3^c		3		8
Nic	11	8			−17	11
Bol	9	9			2	−8
Ecu	8	8			9	10
Per	2	3	−1		8	11
Phi	−38	−38			−43	−30
Tai	−15	−15			2	−58
SK	87	87			n.a.	89
SAr	44	44	−9	−3		(44)
Bur	16	28	−11	−7		16
Cey	−1	17	−91	−10		−1
Ind	−79	22	−136	1	11	−79
Pak	−135		183			−124
Irq	191	8	14	−4^c		191
Lby	10		114	−5		10
Ins	148	39			−94	54

(continued)

APPENDIX TABLE B-VII (concluded)

Lenders (holders of currencies)	Borrowers (currencies held)					
	Total Currency Holdings	US Dollar Reserves	UK Sterling Reserves	Other[a] Currencies	Gold	Total Gold and Currencies
Group 4 Independent (cont.)						
Tha	78	95	−19	2	−5	73
Eth	36	16	−1	21	3	39
Irn	−141	12	−153[d]		−2	−143
Sud	22		7	15[c]		22
Par	2	2				2
Egy	−354	−25	−331	2	122	−232
Syr	−14	16		−30	14	—
Group 4 Dependencies	2,236	13	1,878	345	62	2,298
UKOT	2,124	5	1,889	230		2,124
WAf	809		809			809
EAf, CAf, & Ade	303		316	−13[c]		303
Mal area	556	2	554			556
HK	162	−25	187			162
WHem	171	11	160			171
Oth & Una	123	17	106			123
Una Dominion and Colonial securities included in £ Reserves	—		−243	243		
BelC	144	30	3	111	63	207
NthOT	18	14		4	−1	17
FrOT & PorOT	−50	−36	−14	n.a.	n.a.	(−50)
IMF, IBRD, UN	134	336	−117	−85	289	423

NOTES TO APPENDIX TABLE B-VII

a Other currencies consist of net changes in Continental OEEC currencies 461 (deposits with BIS, otherwise mainly holdings of OEEC countries and dependencies); Canadian dollars −41 (mainly US and UK); RSA 209 (mainly ⊙T holdings of Dominion and Colonial securities); IBRD bonds 81 (for breakdown, see Appendix Table B-II, note *k*); miscellaneous 17.

b Included in OEEC currencies (other currencies).

c Including changes in, or repatriation of, foreign coin and paper currency held in official institutions and banks, or in circulation.

d The reduction in Iranian Sterling balances (−153) is the residual of the UK figure for the "Other" Area. Iran reports only −58, but for solar years ending March 20. In the year ending March 20, 1950, a large reduction is reported, however, which partly or mainly may have taken place in early 1950. The UK residual figure was, therefore, assumed mainly to refer to Iran, although it includes any changes in Soviet Bloc Sterling holdings.

n.a. = not available.

NOTE: If there is an increase, there is no sign before the figure; if a decrease, a minus sign. See the List of Abbreviations at the end of Appendix B.

Discrepancies: The total increase in currency holdings of 6,942 in this table falls short by 274 of the total increase in liabilities reported by the reserve countries; *viz.:* United States 122, United Kingdom 141, Other 11.

Comparisons to other series: Currency Reserves — IMF, *International Reserves and Liquidity*, Washington, 1958, Appendix Table 3 shows 4,400 plus coverage differences of 1,786 to total 6,186. Difference with Appendix Table B-VII: −586 or 9 per cent, resulting mainly from the inclusion of correspondent accounts, and the exclusion of payments agreements balances in Appendix Table B-VII.

Gold Reserves — Appendix Table B-VII shows 1,930: the *Federal Res. Bulletin* (Dec., 1956) shows 1,960; and IMF, *International Financial Statistics*, Dec., 1954 and Feb., 1956 (rounded figures) shows 2,000.

Statistical Notes to Appendix B

IMF, *Balance of Payments Yearbook,* Washington, annually, mainly Volumes 5–8.

SUPPLEMENTARY SOURCES

United States (U.S. Department of Commerce, unless otherwise specified) – General: *Survey of Current Business* (Supplement), "Balance of Payments of the U.S. 1919–53" (1954); *SCB*, June 1956, pp. 24–31: *SCB* Supplement "Balance of Payments of the U.S., 1949–51"; *SCB* Supplement "Balance of Payments" (1958 and 1963). Aid: *Foreign Transactions of the U.S. Government, Foreign Aid*, April 1952, Tables 9 and 10; *Foreign Grants and Credits by the U.S. Government*, December 1953, 1954, 1955, Tables 6 and 7; *Export-Import Bank of Washington: Semi-Annual Reports to Congress*, July–December 1949–54; *Statistical Abstract of the U.S. 1956*, Table 1112. Portfolio: U.S. Treasury Department, *Treasury Bulletin*, June 1955, Section II, Tables 3 and 4. Direct Investment: *Balance of Payments* (*SCB* Supplement 1963); *SCB*, January 1954, pp. 5–10; *SCB*, August 1956, pp. 14–24; The Petroleum Publishing Company, *Oil and Gas Journal*, December 1954, 1955. Short-Term: U.S. Treasury Department, *Treasury Bulletin*, April 1955, July 1956, Section II, 2; and July 1956, Section I, 2 (banks); May 1950, June 1951, Section II, 4; March 1955, Section IV, 4 (brokers); July 1952–56, Section IV, 1 (nonfinancial concerns). Information and breakdowns not otherwise available were obtained from Mr. Samuel Pizer and Mr. Eugene S. Kerber, whose cooperation is gratefully acknowledged.

United Kingdom – H.M. Treasury, *United Kingdom Balance of Payments 1946–1957,* London, 1959; Cmd. 9119, 9291; Bank of England, *United Kingdom Overseas Investments*, annually; Midland Bank, Ltd., *Press Release on New Capital Issue Statistics,* January 1, 1955, and *Midland Bank Review.*

France – Ministère de Finance, *Balance de Payements entre la Zone Franc et les Pays Etrangers*, annually.

Germany – *Monthly Report of the Deutsche Bundesbank,* particularly June 1961, pp. 42–43.

Canada – Dominion Bureau of Statistics, *The Canadian Balance of International Payments in the Post-War Years, 1946–1952,* Ottawa, 1953; *The Canadian Balance of International Payments and International Investment Position,* annually (1953–58).

Australia—Commonwealth Bureau of Census and Statistics, *Annual Bulletin of Overseas Investment 1957–58 with Comparative Data for Previous Years from 1947–48*, New Series No. 3, Canberra.

India—Reserve Bank of India, *Report on the Survey of India's Foreign Liabilities and Assets as on 31st December 1953*, Bombay, 1955; *Report, as on 31st December 1955*, Bombay, 1957.

Iraq—Regional distribution of petroleum investment estimated by Cornelius Dwyer for NBER.

New Zealand—Department of Statistics, *Report on the Official Estimates of Balance of Payments for the Year 1950–51; ... for the Year 1954–55; ... for the Year 1957–58*, Wellington.

South Africa—South Africa Reserve Bank, *The Foreign Liabilities and Assets of the Union of South Africa, Final Results of the 1956 Census* (Suppl. to *Quarterly Bulletin of Statistics,* December 1958).

Mexico—U.S. Department of Commerce, *Investment in Mexico*, Washington, 1955, p. 11, Table 16; Comision de la CNIT, *Estudio General sobre las Inversiones Extranjeras I*, Mexico, 1955, p. 18, Table 3.

Venezuela—Banco Central de Venezuela, *Memoria,* 1953 and 1957; regional distribution of petroleum investment estimated by Cornelius Dwyer for NBER.

Israel—Central Bureau of Statistics and Economic Research of Israel, *Balance of Payments Report* (Falk Report), 1957; *International Financial News Service,* Vol. III, 27; IV, 20, 26, 42; V, 12, 31, Washington (IMF).

Japan—The Bank of Japan, The Foreign Research Society, *Statistical Data and List of Principal Cases of Foreign Capital Investment in Japan,* annually.

Dependent Overseas Territories—General source: OEEC, *Economic Development of Overseas Countries and Territories Associated with OEEC Member Countries*, Paris, 1958. UKOT: Cmd. 8243, 8253, 8553, 8856, 9169, 9489 (grants and portfolio issues). FrOT: OEEC source, Table 44, p. 108; OEEC, *6th Report of the OEEC*, Vol. II, Table 53, p. 231 and pp. 251–3, Paris, 1955. PorOT: OEEC source, Tables 16, 18, pp. 190–1.

Nonterritorial Organizations—BIS: IMF, *International Reserves and Liquidity*, Washington, 1958, Appendix Table 3 (Continental deposits); IMF, *International Financial Statistics*, February 1954, 1956 (reserve tables); *Federal Reserve Bulletins* (gold). EPU: IMF, *International Financial Statistics*, EPU tables 1950–54; *Federal Reserve Bulletin* (gold). IBRD: IMF, *International Financial Statistics*, February 1956,

IBRD table; IBRD, *Annual Reports;* breakdowns and information not otherwise available were obtained from the staff of the IBRD, whose cooperation is gratefully acknowledged. IMF: IMF, *International Financial Statistics,* February 1956, IMF tables; IMF, *Annual Reports; Federal Reserve Bulletin* (gold).

List of Abbreviations

Ade	Aden	Cey	Ceylon
Af	Africa	Chi	Chile
Afg	Afghanistan	COEEC	Continental OEEC
Alg	Algeria	Col	Colombia
Ant	Antilles	COT	Continental Overseas
Arg	Argentina		Territories
Asl	Australia	CR	Costa Rica
AslOT	Australian Overseas	Cub	Cuba
	Territories	Cyp	Cyprus
Aus	Austria		
		Den	Denmark
Bel	Belgium including	Dom	Dominican Republic
	Luxembourg		
BelC	Belgian Congo in-	EAf	British East Africa
	cluding Ruanda-	ECA	Economic Coopera-
	Urundi (Belgian		tion Administration
	Overseas Territories)	ECCS	European Communi-
Ber	Berlin		ty for Coal and Steel
BIS	Bank for Interna-	Ecu	Ecuador
	tional Settlements	EEur	Eastern European
Bol	Bolivia		Countries
Bor	Borneo	Egy	Egypt
Bra	Brazil	ElS	El Salvador
BrG	British Guiana	EPU	European Payments
BrH	British Honduras		Union
Bur	Burma	Eth	Ethiopia
BWI	British West Indies	Eur	Europe
		EurI	European Institutions
CAf	Central Africa		(IEPA or EPU, BIS,
CAm	Central America		and ECCS)
Can	Canada	EXIM	Export Import Bank

FE	Far East	Jam	Jamaica
Fin	Finland	Jor	Jordan
Fr	France	Jpn	Japan
FrOT	French Overseas Territories		
		Ken	Kenya
		Kor	Korea
GC	Gold Coast		
Ger	Germany		
Gr	Greece	LA	Latin America
Gua	Guatemala	Leb	Lebanon
		Lib	Liberia
		Lby	Libya
Hai	Haiti		
HK	Hong Kong		
Hon	Honduras	Mal	Malaya
		ME	Middle East
IBRD	International Bank for Reconstruction and Development	Mex	Mexico
		Mis	Miscellaneous
		Mor	Morocco
		MSA	Mutual Security Agency
Ice	Iceland		
Ich	Indochina		
IEPA	Intra-European Payments Agreement	Nep	Nepal
IIAA	Institute of Inter-American Affairs	Nic	Nicaragua
		Nig	Nigeria
		Nor	Norway
IMF	International Monetary Fund	NR	Northern Rhodesia
Ind	India	Nth	Netherlands
Ins	Indonesia	NthOT	Dutch Overseas Territories
IntI	International Institutions (UN, IBRD, IMF)	NtO	Nonterritorial Organizations (UN, IMF, IBRD, IEPA, EPU, ECCS, BIS)
Ire	Ireland		
Irn	Iran		
IRO	International Refugee Organization	Nya	Nyasaland
		NZ	New Zealand
Irq	Iraq		
Isr	Israel	OECD	Organization for Economic Cooperation and Development
Ita	Italy		
ItS	Italian Somali		

OEEC	Organization of the European Economic Community	Swi	Switzerland
		Syr	Syria
OOT	Other Overseas Territories	Tai	Taiwan
		Tha	Thailand
OSBl	Other Soviet Bloc countries	Tur	Turkey
Oth	Other	Uga	Uganda
		UK	United Kingdom
Pak	Pakistan	UKOT	United Kingdom Overseas Territories
Pal	Palestine		
Pan	Panama	UN	United Nations
Par	Paraguay	Una	Unallocated
Per	Peru	Uni	Unidentified
Phi	Philippines	UNICEF	United Nations Children's Fund
Por	Portugal		
PorOT	Portuguese Overseas Territories	UNKRA	United Nations Korean Relief
		UNRWA	United Nations Palestine Refugees
RFd	Rhodesian Federation		
RSA	Rest of Sterling Area	Uru	Uruguay
RyI	Ryukyu Islands	US	United States
		USSR	Union of Soviet Socialist Republics
SA	Sterling Area		
SAf	South Africa	Ven	Venezuela
SAr	Saudi Arabia		
SBl	Soviet Bloc		
Sin	Singapore	WAf	British West Africa
SK	South Korea	WEur	Western Europe
Sp	Spain	WHem	Western Hemisphere
SR	Southern Rhodesia		
Sud	Sudan	Yug	Yugoslavia
Swe	Sweden		

INDEX

Aden, capital flow figures for, 98, 119, 136

Afghanistan, 26
  capital flow figures, 73, 98
  classification by area, 88

Algeria, classification by area, 87

Antilles, capital flow figures for, 93

Area system
  by economic level and trade orientation, 18–19, 84–89
  and IMF, 17, 18n, 57n

Argentina, 56
  capital flow figures, 71, 93–94, 95, 97, 105, 111, 117, 123, 130, 134
  classification by area, 85

Australia, 27, 29, 46, 52n, 53
  capital flow figures, 71, 94, 97–99, 104, 111, 115–19, 123, 134

Australian overseas territories, 27
  capital flow figures, 119

Austria
  capital flow figures, 92, 101, 102, 109, 115, 122, 123, 129, 133
  classification by area, 19, 84

Bank for International Settlements, 18n, 39n, 99, 102, 131, 133

Behrman, Jack, 53n

Belgian Congo (including Ruanda-Burundi), 30n, 34, 50, 52n
  capital flow figures, 73, 99, 113, 119, 124, 136

Belgium (including Luxembourg), 33, 34, 35
  capital flow figures, 92–94, 99, 102, 105, 109, 111, 113, 115–19, 122, 123, 127, 129, 133
  classification by area, 19, 61n, 84

Berlin, 104

Bolivia
  capital flow figures, 72, 97, 124, 127, 135
  classification by area, 87

Borneo, capital flow figures for, 101

Brazil, 49n, 55, 56, 58–59
  capital flow figures, 71, 77, 94, 95, 96, 99, 103, 105, 112, 115, 117, 123, 127, 130, 134
  classification by area, 86

British East Africa, capital flow figures for, 98, 136

British Guiana, classification by area, 88

British Honduras, classification by area, 89

British West Africa, 59, 60
  capital flow figures, 98, 136

British West Indies, capital flow figures for, 98

Burma
  capital flow figures, 72, 97, 118, 127, 135
  classification by area, 87

Cairncross, A. K., 76n

Canada, 21, 22, 32, 42, 43, 44, 46, 48, 51–52, 53, 54, 65, 75, 76
  capital flow figures, 71, 92–100, 101, 109, 110, 112, 113, 115–21, 122, 123, 134
  classification by area, 85